ENGLAND

England

John Burningham

Jonathan Cape

LONDON

John Burningham would like to thank
Tom Maschler for his belief in E N G L A N D,
Paul Welti for his work on E N G L A N D and everyone
who has painstakingly researched and contributed
material to the book.

First published in Great Britain in 1992 by
Jonathan Cape Ltd, 20 Vauxhall Bridge Road, London SW1V 2SA
Colour origination by Dot Gradations, Chelmsford, Essex
Printed and bound in Great Britain by Butler & Tanner Ltd, Frome and London
A CIP record for this title is available from the British Library

ISBN 0 224 03161 9

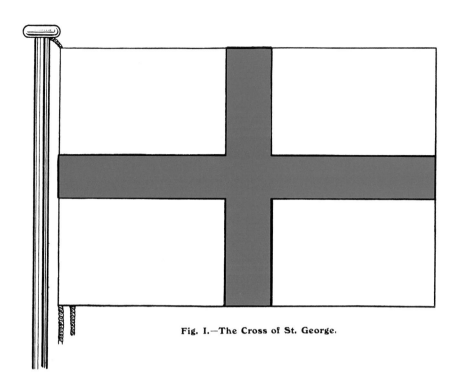

Fig. I.—The Cross of St. George.

The Origin and Meaning of Our Flag.

YOU have all heard of St. George and the Dragon. St. George, like many other saints and warriors, had a special emblem or badge which was carried by those men who chose St. George as their patron saint. It was a broad red cross on a white ground, and you will see a picture of it in Fig. 1.

In the days of the Crusades, English soldiers often used to wear a badge like this on their arm, or decorated the front of their fighting dress with this emblem, so that by degrees St. George became recognised as the Patron Saint of England, and St. George's Cross was gradually adopted as the national ensign. We often read in our history and early literature such phrases as "For St. George and Merrie England," "God for Harry, England and St. George," and there is no doubt that as soon as flags became a part of the outfit of an army or of fighting ships the English carried a St. George's Cross as the emblem of England. This simple but grand old flag was used for many years without any change. Edward III. is known to have flown the St. George's Cross at the naval battle of Sluys in 1346, and it was under this flag that Sir Francis Drake, Sir Walter Raleigh, Frobisher, Hawkins and Howard sailed on their adventurous voyages, or fought the Spaniards under good Queen Bess.

BY

CECIL H. CROFTS, M.A.,

AUTHOR OF "BRITAIN ON AND BEYOND THE SEA."

Win Through.

NO ! Clouds won't for ever be dull and grey

For sooner or later they'll pass away,

And then once again will come peeping through

A patch of bright colour–heaven's own blue.

So when trials come fast, and life seems all wrong,

Hold yourself well in hand, they can't last long.

Just keep a stiff lip and lift up your chin

If you've courage enough you're bound to win.

Mr. Ivan Lawrence (Burton): Is my right hon. Friend aware that there was unnecessary chaos in the section of the M6 that leads to Corley service station on Saturday? I was stationary for 18 hours, fortunately in the company of my wife and with a certain amount of good Burton beer that I keep with me for emergencies. But there can be no excuse for the authorities not closing the M6 when they saw the trouble that was happening. The trouble had clearly begun a good hour or so before I joined the motorway. There was no gritting of any sort. There were no snowploughs.

I did not see a police officer for 15 hours, and when one arrived he had no idea what was happening. No attempt was made to release the traffic that had been travelling eastward towards the M1 to the entirely empty opposite side of the M6 until 2 am. That reveals a disgraceful lack of co-ordination among local authorities, the police and whoever else may be responsible. Will my right hon. Friend look into that? There are still hundreds of vehicles in the area. Goodness knows how many of those in them were diabetic, unwell or old, who had no access to lavatories and telephones. The whole thing was disgraceful. The shortcomings could be corrected if my right hon. Friend were to devote his attention to ensuring that there is no lack of co-ordination in future.

Mr. Baker: I shall draw the remarks of my hon. and learned Friend to the attention of the chief constables in the areas that he mentioned, including the way in which traffic was controlled. My hon. and learned Friend underlined the idea that was put to me earlier by a chief constable, which was that when those difficulties occur, consideration should be given to early closure of the motorways. I hasten to add that I refer to those that are in urban areas. It would be much more difficult to close those that are in more remote rural areas.

I am sure that my hon. and learned Friend's journey, with his wife, was necessary. The chief constable of Thames Valley has told me, however, that his officers dug out quite a few elderly people from their cars on Saturday. Those people, having seen that it was a snowy day, had gone out for a run.

Extract from Hansard, 10 December 1990, C. 665, 666. Hansard is the Official Report of the House of Lords and House of Commons Debates and is Parliamentary Copyright.

John Peel.

IN SPRINGTIME.

IT was a lover and his lass,
　　With a hey and a ho, and a hey nonny no,
That o'er the green cornfield did pass,
　　In springtime, the only pretty ring-time,
　　When birds do sing, hey ding a ding, ding,
　　Sweet lovers love the spring.

This carol they began that hour,
　　With a hey and a ho, and a hey nonny no,
How that life is but a flower,
　　　In springtime, &c.

And therefore take the present time,
　　With a hey and a ho, and a hey nonny no,
For love is crownèd with the prime,
　　　In springtime, &c.

SHAKESPEARE.

As You Like It *(Act V, Scene iii), William Shakespeare*

CRUFTS
ROLL OF HONOUR
Best in Show Winners

1928	Greyhound	Ch Primley Sceptre	M. Whitley
1929	Scottish Terrier	Heather Necessity	E. Chapman
1930	Cocker Spaniel	Luckystar of Ware	H. S. Lloyd
1931	Cocker Spaniel	Luckystar of Ware	H. S. Lloyd
1932	Labrador Retriever	Bramshaw Bob	Lorna Countess Howe
1933	Labrador Retriever	Bramshaw Bob	Lorna Countess Howe
1934	Greyhound	Southball Moonstone	B. Harland Worden
1935	Pointer	Pennine Prima Donna	A. Eggleston
1936	Chow Chow	Ch Choonam Hung Kwong	Mrs V. A. M. Mannooch
1937	Labrador Retriever	Ch Cheveralla Ben of Banchory	Lorna Countess Howe
1938	Cocker Spaniel	Exquisite Model of Ware	H. S. Lloyd
1939	Cocker Spaniel	Exquisite Model of Ware	H. S. Lloyd
1948	Cocker Spaniel	Tracey Witch of Ware	H. S. Lloyd
1950	Cocker Spaniel	Tracey Witch of Ware	H. S. Lloyd
1951	Welsh Terrier	Twynstar Dyma-Fi	Capt & Mrs I. M. Thomas
1952	Bulldog	Ch Noways Chuckles	J. T. Barnard
1953	Great Dane	Ch Elch Elder of Ouborough	W. G. Siggers
1955	Standard Poodle	Ch Tzigane Aggri of Nashend	Mrs A. Proctor
1956	Greyhound	Treetops Golden Falcon	Mrs W. De Casembroot & Miss H. Greenish
1957	Keeshond	Ch Volkrijk of Vorden	Mrs I. M. Tucker
1958	Pointer	Ch Chiming Bells	Mrs W. Parkinson
1959	Welsh Terrier	Ch Sandstorm Saracen	Mesdames Leach & Thomas
1960	Irish Wolfhound	Sulhamstead Merman	Mrs Nagle & Miss Clark
1961	Airedale Terrier	Ch Riverina Tweedsbairn	Miss P. McCaughey & Mrs D. Schutch
1962	Wire Fox Terrier	Ch Crackwyn Cockspur	H. L. Gill
1963	Lakeland Terrier	Rogerholm Recruit	W. Rogers
1964	English Setter	Sh Ch Silbury Soames of Madavale	Mrs A. Williams
1965	Alsatian (GSD)	Ch Fenton of Kentwood	Miss S. H. Godden
1966	Toy Poodle	Oakington Puckshill Amber Sunblush	Mrs C. E Perry
1967	Lakeland Terrier	Ch Stingray of Derryabah	Mr & Mrs Postlewaite
1968	Dalmatian	Ch Fanhill Faune	Mrs E. J. Woodyatt
1969	Alsatian (GSD)	Ch Hendrawen's Nibelung of Charavigne	Mr & Mrs E. J. White
1970	Pyrenean Mountain Dog	Bergerie Knur	Mr & Mrs F. S. Prince
1971	Alsatian (GSD)	Ch Ramacon Swashbuckler	Prince Ahmed Hussain
1972	Bull Terrier	Ch Abraxas Audacity	Miss V. Drummond-Dick
1973	Cavalier King Charles Spaniel	Alansmere Aquarius	Messrs Hall & Evans
1974	St Bernard	Ch Burtonswood Bossy Boots	Miss M. Hinds
1975	Wire Fox Terrier	Ch Brookewire Brandy of Layven	Messrs Bernelli & Dondina
1976	West Highland White Terrier	Ch Dianthus Buttons	Mrs K. Newstead
1977	English Setter	Bournemouth Dancing Master	G. F. Williams
1978	Wire Fox Terrier	Ch Harrowhill Huntsman	Miss E. Howles
1979	Kerry Blue Terrier	Eng Am Ch Callaghan of Leander	Miss W. Streatfield
1980	Flat-Coat Retriever	Ch Shargleam Blackcap	Miss P. Chapman
1981	Irish Setter	Ch Astley's Portia of Rua	Mrs & Miss Tuite
1982	Toy Poodle	Ch Grayco Hazlenut	Mrs L. A. Howard
1983	Afghan Hound	Ch Montravia Kaskarak Hitari	Mrs P. Gibbs
1984	Lhasa Apso	Ch Saxonsprings Hackensack	Mrs J. Blyth
1985	Poodle (Standard)	Ch Montravia Tommy-Gun	Miss M. Gibbs
1986	Airedale Terrier	Ch Ginger Christmas Carol	Miss A. Livraghi
1987	Afghan Hound	Ch Viscount Grant	Mr & Mrs C. Amoo
1988	English Setter	Sh Ch Starlite Express at Valsett	Mr & Mrs J. W. Watkin
1989	Bearded Collie	Ch Potterdale Classic of Moonhill	Mrs B. White
1990	West Highland White Terrier	Ch Olac Moon Pilot	D. Tattersall
1991	Clumber Spaniel	Sh Ch Raycroft Socialite	R. Dunne
1992	Whippet	Ch Pencloe Dutch Cold	Miss M. Bolton

Reproduced by kind permission of The Kennel Club.

No.	Date	MP CP GTH	MP CP No.	Div	STATION / G.T.M. NAME	ADDRESS	Date	BREED	COLOUR	Sex	C	DA
2550	21 Feb	11	69	P	CATFORD	Rushey Green SE6	21	mongrel	Blk Brn	D		
2551	11		24	M	EAST DULWICH	Herne Hill SE24	21	X BEAGLE	TM	D		6
2552	44		23	W	TOOTING	Garratt Lane	21	Greyhound	Bl Wht	D		
2553	9		44	R	GREENWICH	Plumstead SE18	21	X LABRADOR	Blk Tan	B		10
2554	87		10	P	CHISLEHURST	Chislehurst	20	mongrel	TM	D		
2555	8		63	R	ELTHAM	Plumstead	21	mongrel	Brn Wht	B		
2556	21		23	M	EAST DULWICH	SE22	21	mongrel	Blk Tan	D		
2557	1		34	R	WOOLWICH	Brewery Rd	21	STAFF	Blk	B		05
2558	2		28	R	SHOOTERS Hill	Mottingham	21	mongrel	Wht Brn	B		13
2559	23		7	A	WANSTEAD	o/s Sainsbury	21	X DOBERMANN	Grey Brn	D		
2560	14		12	A	LEYTONSTONE	o/s Beaconfield Rd	21	mongrel	Blk Tan	D		7
2561	12		7	A	ILFORD	Chelmsford Gdns	21	mongrel	Blk Wht	D		
2562	13		62	G	HACKNEY	Wells St E9	22	mongrel	Brn	D		18
2563	25			CP	BISHOPSGATE	Moorgate	22	mongrel	Brindle	D		
2564	41		27	K	HORNCHURCH	o/s Upminster Stn	20	mongrel	Blk Tan	B		
2565	4		13	A	LEYTON	E.11	22	DOBERMANN	Blk Brn	B	25/2	
2566	4		24	A	CHADWELL HTH	Ilford B.R.	22	E. BULL	Wht	B	25/2	
2567	9		61	G	HACKNEY	Queensbridge Rd	21	G S D	Blk Tan	D		17
2568	85		14	H	LEMAN ST	Tarling St	22	mongrel	Blk Brn	B		
2569	15		60	G	HACKNEY	Kingsmead Way	21	mongrel	Tan	B		
2570	1		8	E	HOLBORN	Grays Inn Rd	21	mongrel	Blk Brindle	B	24/2	
2571	1		78	A	WALTHAM ABBEY	Monks Way	21	mongrel	Tan	B	27/2	
2572	9		48	H	TOTTENHAM	Fore St N9	21	mongrel	Blk Wht	D		
2573	2		29	A	CHINGFORD	Slug + Kettle P/H	21	mongrel	Tan	D	23/2	
2574	32		22	Y	ST ANNS RD	Eckington Ho	21	mongrel	Blk Tan	D		26
2575	12		21	Y	ST ANNS RD	" "	21	X LABRADOR	Blk Tan	D		
2576	16		13	E	ALBANY ST	Euston Undergr	21	mongrel	Brn Wht	D		
2577	1		12	E	ALBANY ST	Gt Portland St NW1	21	mongrel	Brn	B	27/2	
2578	11		34	E	KENTISH TWN	Swains Lane N6	21	mongrel	Sandy Wht	B		4
2579	21			N	HIGHBURY	St Marys Ave E13	21	mongrel	Tan Wht Blk	D		
2580	9		28	N	HOLLOWAY	Caledonian Rd	21	X LABRADOR	Blk	D		
2581	105		16	Y	CHESHUNT	o/s the drive	21	X DOBERMANN	Choc Wht	D		6
2582	4		47	Y	TOTTENHAM	White Hart Lane	21	POODLE	Wht	D		4
2583	11		30	X	SOUTHALL	Carlyle Ave	19	mongrel	Sable	D		

The Dogs Home Battersea
4 Battersea Park Road, London SW8 4AA
Telephone: 01-622 3626

REMARKS
R.S.P.C.A
Ret 12/5/89
collar
collar
chain
collar
collar
Nervous
BM 28/3/89
RET 17/5 collar
Serum collar
P.F
collar
O.D
O.D
482 1570
collar
R.S.P.C.A Holloway
collar
TO B/M 21/3/89

The author and publishers gratefully acknowledge the kind permission of The Dogs Home, Battersea to reproduce copyright material. The artist would like to make clear that the above picture is his own interpretation, and is in no way intended to document actual conditions at The Dogs Home.

Four and Eight   No 48
No 22   Dinky Do
       Eight and Five No. 85
No 13 Unlucky for some.
       The Brighton Line No 59
No. 11 Legs Eleven.
         Five and Six No 56
         Six and Two   No 62
No 10   Maggies Den.
       Two fat ladies No 88
       All the threes   No 33
No 39 All the steps
        On its own No 1
       Three and Two No 32
No 57 All the beans
        One little duck No 2
No 21. The key of the door.

HOW TO PASS AND RECEIVE A TELEPHONE CALL.

PASSING A CALL.

Before passing a call to the Exchange the subscriber should wait until he hears the telephonist's "Number, please?" and then, speaking CLEARLY and DISTINCTLY, with the lips **almost touching the mouthpiece,** he should state the number required.

FIRST the name of the Exchange and THEN the number.

The method of pronouncing numbers in Telephone Exchanges has been devised to guard as far as possible against inaccuracies and a description of the system may be of assistance to subscribers.

It is important to remember that the distinctive sounds of consonants become blurred in the transmission of speech by telephone and words containing the same vowels are apt to sound alike. Greater care is therefore necessary in speaking by telephone than is required in ordinary speech, if mistakes are to be avoided.

0 is pronounced as **"OH,"** with long "O."

1 ,, ,, **"WUN,"** emphasizing the consonant "N."

2 ,, ,, **"TOO,"** emphasizing the consonant "T" and with long "OO."

3 ,, ,, **"THR-R-EE,"** with slightly rolling "R" and long "E."

4 ,, ,, **"FOER,"** one syllable with long "O."

5 ,, ,, **"FIFE,"** emphasizing the consonants "F."

6 ,, ,, **"SIX,"** with long "X."

7 ,, ,, **"SEV-EN,"** two syllables.

8 ,, ,, **"ATE,"** with long "A" and emphasizing the consonant "T."

9 ,, ,, **"NINE,"** one syllable with long "I" and emphasizing the consonants "N."

ANSWERING A CALL.

The call should be answered promptly.

On taking off the receiver, the called subscriber should not say "Hullo!" or "Who's there?" but should immediately announce his name.

A householder would say : "Mr. Thomas Brown speaking."

The maidservant : "Mr. Brown's house."

Mr. Brown, at his office, would say : "Brown & Co., Mr. Thomas Brown speaking."

His clerk : "Brown & Co."

FINISH OF CONVERSATION.

The receiver should be replaced immediately the conversation is finished. Subscribers having Private Branch Exchange switchboards should ensure that adequate arrangements are made for **PROMPT DISCONNECTION AT THE SWITCHBOARD.** Neglect to do this may result in serious inconvenience.

GENERAL POST OFFICE.   *October,* 1923.

(43822) Wt. 11863—S31 675m 9/23 H.St. G.148
(44376) Wt. 15290—G288 125 10/23 H.St. G.148

Emmanuel, and Magdalene,
    And St Catharine's, and St John's,
Are the dreariest places,
    And full of dons.

Extract from A Letter to a Shropshire Lad, *by Rupert Brooke, 1911.*

January 29 & 30

FLOWER SHOW

including an Ornamental Plant Competition and exhibits of botanical paintings.

February 19 & 20

FLOWER SHOW

including an Ornamental Plant Competition and exhibits of botanical paintings

March 12 & 13

EARLY SPRING SHOW

including the Early Camellia and Early Rhododendron Competitions and Magnolia and Ornamental Plant Competition.

April 9 & 10

SPRING FLOWER SHOW

including the Main Camellia Competition, Daffodil Show, Ornamental Plant and Sewell Medal Competitions.

April 30 & May 1

FLOWER SHOW

including the Main Rhododendron Competition, Ornamental Tree & Shrub Competition, Late Daffodil Competition and Tulip Competition.

June 19 & 20

THE EARLY SUMMER SHOW

including a Flowering Tree and Shrub Competition and competitions organised by *The British Iris Society*, *The National Carnation Society*, and *The Delphinium Society*.

July 17 & 18

FLOWER SHOW

including a Summer Fruit and Vegetable Competition, Hardy Herbaceous Plant Competition and competition organised by *The National Carnation Society*.

The National Dahlia Society is holding their show on August 29, and *The National Chrysanthemum Society* will be holding their show on November 2 & 3. In addition to the Westminster Shows, *The British Iris Society* is holding a week end show at Wisley on June 2 & 3 and *The Delphinium Society* will be holding a weekend show at Wisley on June 30 & July 1.

Extract from The Royal Horticultural Society Chelsea Flower Show Official Catalogue 1990.

Garden Roller. Old fashioned roller wanted. Minimum diameter roughly 30in. Please write giving dimensions and type of handle and price. Will collect. Member 60193 (Clwyd).

Gent's leather brief case. Good condition. (Not type that expands when being opened and has 2/3 pockets) it appears they are no longer manufactured. Member 10579 (Kent)

Large magnifying glass or 'easy viewer' or similar for reading, sewing etc, glass lens only (no synthetics please). Powerful magnifying mirror. "The Foxes Frolic or a Day with the Topsy Turvy Hounds", by Sir Francis Burnand – and illustrations Harry B. Neilson, published William Collins early this century. Member 40010 (Somerset)

Croquet Mallet in good condition for enthusiast. Also hoops, balls, post, in fact croquet set. Please state price. Member 123314 (Oxon)

White line marker for young boys' football team just starting up. Member 127008 (London)

Does any member have a dusty unused unwanted book 'Rambles Round Brandford' by William Cudworth (approx 1910). Somebody borrowed mine!! I have an old Coronet box camera I no longer need. No reasonable offer turned down Member 116256 (W Yorks).

A Mehe-Maija Stainless. Member 91564 (Cumbria)

78 Gramophone. Portable wind-up wanted to replace old friend mistaken for bomb, now sorely missed on picnics! Must be in full working order. Member 121055 (London)

Royal Crown Derby – Redaues – large meat dish, vegetable dishes, and any other oddments for dinner service please. Member 129756 (W Sussex)

Common Blood by C.E. Hanscomb. Printed by The Queen Anne Press Ltd. Member 119601 (Herts).

Wedgwood – "Ice Rose" side plates – other dinner service items considered. Member 81291 (Staffs)

Blue Moon crockery by Poole Potteries, and also stainless steel cutlery by Elkington. All items required to meet the needs of a growing family. Member 117243 (Herts)

Letters, documents etc with wax impressions of seals, wanted by collector. Condition immaterial providing wax seal intact. Member 97072 (Derby)

Old Hunting Trophy wanted by member furnishing large 16th Century house – especially stuffed tiger's head or mounted horns. Good price paid for interesting or unusual example. Need not be in perfect condition as restoration or repair can be arranged. Copy of Millers Gardener's Dictionary in any condition also wanted. Member 122670 (Norwich)

Arabic conversation language course. Member 111597 (Gloucs)

Long mattress (6ft 6in to 7ft 0in) plus bed if available, for member's huge son. Member 103405 (Wilts).

Zeiss, Leitz, Ross or similar binoculars, in unservicable, poor, or bad condition, even very incomplete. Member 74393 (Oxon)

By E.M. Delafield: First Love; The Optimist; Women Are Like That; Mrs Harter; The Chip and The Block; The Entertainment; Heel of Achilles; A Suburban Young Man; Zella Sees Herself; Jill; The Pelicans; Reversion to Type, Messauna of The Suburbs. Member 118494 (Worcs).

Is there a model kit enthusiast who could assemble and paint a wooden dolls house for my daughter? I had no idea there were so many little bits and no instructions – only a picture and diagram of the finished article! Member 128252 (London)

Needlework Box and Fire Screen required for soft furnishing student. Member 127722 (Warks/Leics)

A 1974 Edition of Halycon Days Enamel St. Valentine's Day Box. A Wooden Roller Front Cabinet. with pull out drawers. Member 124726 (W. Midlands)

Retired Photographer seeks: Any older Leica camera with Elmar lens. Stereo viewer. Projector for 6x9cm transparencies ('memory lane' stuff, used when starting business 40 years ago). Member 126180 (Oxford)

Wedgwood 'Penshurst' cups, saucers, side plates, cereal bowls or pudding plates. Member 109973 (Perth)

Old croquet set in good condition. Also old porcelain figurine or dinner service suitable for wedding present. Member 140442 (Oxon)

CLOTHES • FURS JEWELS

6th D.C.O. Lancers, Indian Cavalry. Member wishes to purchase up to one complete set S.D. uniform Regt brass buttons for use not re-sale. Member 83508 (Devon).

Light (Summer) weight suits, formal or informal, for man ht 6ft, ch 44in, w 40in, il 32in, good condition. S.A.E. secures reply, approval against postage. Member 65939 (Wilts)

Black Silk Topper in good condition, preferably with box. Member 79858 (N. Lancs)

Extract from Country, *the magazine of the Country Gentlemen's Association, October 1990.*

Telephone: 071-935 2524

169 Harley Street
London, W1N 1DA

1st **July** 1990

Mr. C J Bedenmah
presents his compliments to

J. M. Grubihmann Esq.
....

and begs to state that his fee for
professional services

£ 150. 00

REACH FOR THE NEW SUN

YOUR SUN will be different on Monday. Very different.

But it will still be YOUR kind of newspaper.

It will be in a new, easier-to-handle tabloid form. Smaller pages, but many more of them. It will have lots of new names. Lots of new, exciting ideas.

But the most important thing to remember is that the new Sun will still be the paper that CARES.

The paper that cares—passionately—about truth, and beauty and justice.

Independent, aware

The paper that cares about people. About the kind of world we live in. And about the kind of world we would like our children to live in.

The new Sun will have a conscience. It will never forget its radical traditions. It will be truly independent, but politically mightily aware.

IT WILL never, ever hesitate to speak its mind.

IT WILL never, ever sit on fences.

IT WILL never, ever be boring.

IT WILL, of course, be keeping all that's best about the Sun you know. Lots of familiar features—the popular Pacesetters page, for example—will be there.

The new team

The incomparable TEMPLEGATE, Britain's most famous tipster, will be in the team.

So will brilliant DEIRDRE McSHARRY, the writer who dominates the fashion scene.

Witty, incisive JON AKASS will continue to write for the paper. UNITY HALL, ELIZABETH PROSSER, KEITH MASON, HARRY ARNOLD and lots of other familiar names will appear as usual.

Among the new people helping them to produce the new Sun will be some of the best brains in the business.

They have been flocking to join from all over Britain—and beyond. They recognise that the rebirth of the Sun is the most significant event in publishing for many years.

And just look at some of the things they have been lining up for you.

In the first week alone Sun readers will be offered:

● A series of long extracts from **The Love Machine,** the world's best-selling novel of 1969.

● Inside-soccer stories by the top names —a million pounds' worth of soccer talent.

● The supreme readers' service—your problems answered by the world-famous John Hilton Bureau.

● Opportunities for women to win new CARS, COLOUR TV SETS, and a "NEW-YOU" session at a famous health farm.

● New and original cartoons.

There will always be something new in the new Sun.

Lively, entertaining

We do not promise miracles. Like all other newspapers we have our problems, and we shall have our shortcomings.

What we DO promise is a newspaper which will be the most LIVELY, the most INTERESTING, the most INFORMATIVE and the most ENTERTAINING in the business.

On Monday, reach for the Sun. Stay with the Sun. You'll be glad you did.

RUPERT MURDOCH, Publisher

Extract from the Sun, 15 November 1969.

So the Government's attitude towards the road haulage industry is this. You and we worked together against the threat of nationalisation of road haulage. We won that battle. Now we must show that we were right to win it. What the country needs of us, and has a right to expect, is a vigorous and efficient road haulage industry. Much of what is needed can be provided by you and you alone. I have no doubts myself that you will prove as fully equal to the task in the future as you have been in the past. We in the Government will back you all we can, by providing surely (and not so very slowly) a really first class network of trunk roads on top of the extraordinary dense network of still quite serviceable roads which this country already has. We shall press on with this programme. We shall try to make sure that the roads we have and new roads we build give the best dividend possible by concentrating a good deal of our attention on the traffic problem. Sometimes in this we shall be forced to require some sacrifices by individuals or by groups in the interests of the many. Road haulage will enjoy many of the benefits from improved roads and improved traffic flow. I am sure it will be willing and eager to play its part in co-operating with us in the solution of the traffic problems in our towns and cities.

Extract from a speech given by John Hay to the Road Haulage Association, 18 May 1960.

LONDON
======

A102 LONDON: THE BLACKWALL TUNNEL IS CLOSED SOUTHBOUND FROM 10PM
SATURDAY TO 6AM SUNDAY 28/29TH MARCH.

A3 LONDON: CLAPHAM HIGH STREET DOWN TO 1 LANE SOUTHBOUND NORTH OF
A2217 CLAPHAM PARK ROAD TO LAY A NEW GAS MAIN (STARTED 25TH MARCH,
UNTIL 9TH APRIL).

NORTH
=====

M56 CHESHIRE: CONTRAFLOW J9-J10 (LYMM/NORTHWICH) WITH 2 LANES
EASTBOUND AND DOWN TO 1 LANE WESTBOUND ON APPROACH TO THE CONTRAFLOW.
LINK FROM M6 NORTHBOUND TO M56 WESTBOUND CLOSED WITH DIVERSIONS.

M56 GREATER MANCHESTER: FROM MARCH 27TH A CONTRAFLOW WILL BE IN
OPERATION BETWEEN J3-J4 (A5103 PRINCESS PARKWAY/WYTHENSHAWE).
LONG DELAYS ARE LIKELY.

A580 GREATER MANCHESTER: CONTRAFLOW AT LOWTON ST MARYS, NEAR LEIGH,
BETWEEN LANE HEAD AND GREYHOUND ROUNDABOUT, WITH STRICTLY ENFORCED
40MPH SPEED LIMIT, SEVERE DELAYS ARE LIKELY. (UNTIL JUNE).

A41 CHESHIRE: BOUGHTON HEATH, CHESTER IS CLOSED SOUTHBOUND
BETWEEN THE A51 VICARS CROSS AND THE HOOLE ROUNDABOUT. DIVERSIONS
IN OPERATION.

M1 SOUTH YORKSHIRE: ROADWORKS J34-J35 (TINSLEY/ROTHERHAM), ONLY 2
LANES RUNNING BOTH WAYS, SOUTHBOUND ENTRY SLIP ROAD AT J35 CLOSED.
(UNTIL MID APRIIL).

Extract from The Department of Transport publication, Know Your Traffic Signs.

SEA-FEVER

I MUST down to the seas again, to the lonely sea
    and the sky,
And all I ask is a tall ship and a star to steer her
    by,
And the wheel's kick and the wind's song and the
    white sail's shaking,
And a grey mist on the sea's face and a grey dawn
    breaking.

I must down to the seas again, for the call of the
    running tide
Is a wild call and a clear call that may not be
    denied;
And all I ask is a windy day with tne white clouds
    flying,
And the flung spray and the blown spume, and the
    sea-gulls crying.

I must down to the seas again to the vagrant gypsy
    life,
To the gull's way and the whale's way where the
    wind's like a whetted knife;
And all I ask is a merry yarn from a laughing
    fellow-rover,
And quiet sleep and a sweet dream when the long
    trick's over.

'Sea-Fever' by John Masefield, first published in Salt-Water Ballads, 1902.

AND NOW THE SHIPPING FORECAST ISSUED BY THE METEOROLOGICAL
OFFICE AT 1305 ON MONDAY 20 OCTOBER 1986.

THERE ARE WARNINGS OF GALES IN FORTIES CROMARTY FORTH TYNE
DOGGER GERMAN BIGHT HUMBER THAMES DOVER WIGHT PORTLAND PLYMOUTH
BISCAY FINISTERRE SOLE LUNDY FASTNET IRISH SEA SHANNON ROCKALL
MALIN HEBRIDES BAILEY

THE GENERAL SYNOPSIS AT 0700
LOW WALES 981 EXPECTED SOUTHERN BALTIC 975 BY 0700 TOMORROW.
LOW MOVING RAPIDLY EASTNORTHEAST EXPECTED SHANNON 990 BY SAME
TIME. LOW MOVING STEADILY EAST EXPECTED SOUTHEAST ICELAND 966
BY SAME TIME

THE AREA FORECASTS FOR THE NEXT 24 HOURS

VIKING NORTH UTSIRE SOUTH UTSIRE
SOUTHWESTERLY 4 INCREASING 5 TO 7. SHOWERS GOOD

FORTIES CROMARTY FORTH
SOUTHWEST 4 INCREASING 6 TO GALE 8. SHOWERS. GOOD
TYNE DOGGER
VARIABLE 4 BECOMING WEST OR SOUTHWEST 7 TO SEVERE GALE 9, RAIN
THEN SHOWERS. MODERATE OR GOOD

FISHER
SOUTHWESTERLY 4 INCREASING 6 PERHAPS GALE 8 LATER.
SHOWERS. MODERATE OR GOOD

GERMAN BIGHT
CYCLONIC 6 TO GALE 8 BECOMING WESTERLY. OCCASIONAL RAIN. MODERATE
OR POOR BECOMING GOOD

HUMBER THAMES DOVER
MAINLY WESTERLY 6 TO GALE 8, OCCASIONALLY SEVERE GALE 9 AT FIRST,
BACKING SOUTHWEST LATER. RAIN THEN SHOWERS. MODERATE BECOMING
GOOD

WIGHT PORTLAND PLYMOUTH
WEST BACKING SOUTHWEST 7 TO SEVERE GALE 9. SHOWERS EARLY, RAIN
LATER. MAINLY GOOD BECOMING MODERATE OR POOR

TYNE DOGGER
VARIABLE BECOMING WEST OR SOUTHWEST 7 TO SEVERE GALE 9, RAIN
THEN SHOWERS. MODERATE OR GOOD

HEARTS OF OAK

Come, cheer up, my lads ! 'tis to glory
    we steer,
To add something more to this won-
    derful year,
To honour we call you, not press you
    like slaves,
For who are so free as the sons of the
    waves ?

We ne'er see our foes but we wish 'em
    to stay,
They never see us but they wish us
    away ;
If they run, why, we follow, and run
    'em ashore,
For if they won't fight us we cannot
    do more.

                        Chorus.

Chorus—
    Hearts of oak are our ships,
    Hearts of oak are our men ;
      We always are ready ;
      Steady, boys, steady ;
    We'll fight and we'll conquer again
      and again.

They swear they'll invade us, these terrible foes,
They frighten our women, our children and beaux;
But should their flat bottoms in darkness get o'er,
Still Britons they'll find to receive them on shore.

Chorus.

We'll still make 'em run, and we'll still make 'em sweat,
In spite of the devil and Brussels Gazette;
Then cheer up, my lads, with one heart let us sing,
Our soldiers, our sailors, our statesmen, and King.

Chorus.

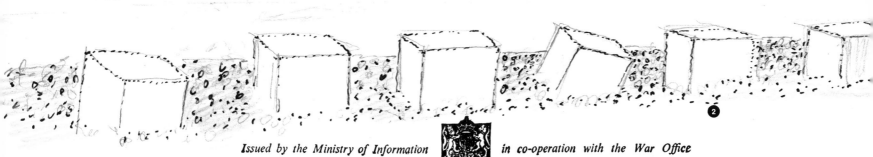

Issued by the Ministry of Information in co-operation with the War Office and the Ministry of Home Security.

If the
INVADER
comes

WHAT TO DO — AND HOW TO DO IT

THE Germans threaten to invade Great Britain. If they do so they will be driven out by our Navy, our Army and our Air Force. Yet the ordinary men and women of the civilian population will also have their part to play. Hitler's invasions of Poland, Holland and Belgium were greatly helped by the fact that the civilian population was taken by surprise. They did not know what to do when the moment came. *You must not be taken by surprise.* This leaflet tells you what general line you should take. More detailed instructions will be given you when the danger comes nearer. Meanwhile, read these instructions carefully and be prepared to carry them out.

I

When Holland and Belgium were invaded, the civilian population fled from their homes. They crowded on the roads, in cars, in carts, on bicycles and on foot, and so helped the enemy by preventing their own armies from advancing against the invaders. You must not allow that to happen here. Your first rule, therefore, is :—

(1) IF THE GERMANS COME, BY PARACHUTE, AEROPLANE OR SHIP, YOU MUST REMAIN WHERE YOU ARE. THE ORDER IS " STAY PUT ".

If the Commander in Chief decides that the place where you live must be evacuated, he will tell you when and how to leave. Until you receive such orders you must remain where you are. If you run away, you will be exposed to far greater danger because you will be machine-gunned from the air as were civilians in Holland and Belgium, and you will also block the roads by which our own armies will advance to turn the Germans out.

II

There is another method which the Germans adopt in their invasion. They make use of the civilian population in order to create confusion and panic. They spread false rumours and issue false instructions. In order to prevent this, you should obey the second rule, which is as follows :—

(2) DO NOT BELIEVE RUMOURS AND DO NOT SPREAD THEM. WHEN YOU RECEIVE AN ORDER, MAKE QUITE SURE THAT IT IS A TRUE ORDER AND NOT A FAKED ORDER. MOST OF YOU KNOW YOUR POLICEMEN AND YOUR A.R.P. WARDENS BY SIGHT, YOU CAN TRUST THEM. IF YOU KEEP YOUR HEADS, YOU CAN ALSO TELL WHETHER A MILITARY OFFICER IS REALLY BRITISH OR ONLY PRETENDING TO BE SO. IF IN DOUBT ASK THE POLICE-MAN OR THE A.R.P. WARDEN. USE YOUR COMMON SENSE.

III

The Army, the Air Force and the Local Defence Volunteers cannot be everywhere at once. The ordinary man and woman must be on the watch. If you see anything suspicious, do not rush round telling your neighbours all about it. Go at once to the nearest policeman, police-station, or military officer and tell them exactly what you saw. Train yourself to notice the exact time and place where you saw anything suspicious, and try to give exact information. Try to check your facts. The sort of report which a military or police officer wants from you is something like this :—

> "At 5.30 p.m. to-night I saw twenty cyclists come into Little Squashborough from the direction of Great Mudtown. They carried some sort of automatic rifle or gun. I did not see anything like artillery. They were in grey uniforms."

Be calm, quick and exact. The third rule, therefore, is as follows :—

(3) KEEP WATCH. IF YOU SEE ANYTHING SUSPICIOUS, NOTE IT CAREFULLY AND GO AT ONCE TO THE NEAREST POLICE OFFICER OR STATION, OR TO THE NEAREST MILITARY OFFICER. DO NOT RUSH ABOUT SPREADING VAGUE RUMOURS. GO QUICKLY TO THE NEAREST AUTHORITY AND GIVE HIM THE FACTS.

IV

Remember that if parachutists come down near your home, they will not be feeling at all brave. They will not know where they are, they will have no food, they will not know where their companions are. They will want you to give them food, means of transport and maps. They will want you to tell them where they have landed, where their comrades are, and where our own soldiers are. The fourth rule, therefore, is as follows :—

(4) DO NOT GIVE ANY GERMAN ANYTHING. DO NOT TELL HIM ANYTHING. HIDE YOUR FOOD AND YOUR BICYCLES. HIDE YOUR MAPS. SEE THAT THE ENEMY GETS NO PETROL. IF YOU HAVE A CAR OR MOTOR BICYCLE, PUT IT OUT OF ACTION WHEN NOT IN USE. IT IS NOT ENOUGH TO REMOVE THE IGNITION KEY; YOU MUST MAKE IT USELESS TO ANYONE EXCEPT YOURSELF.

IF YOU ARE A GARAGE PROPRIETOR, YOU MUST WORK OUT A PLAN TO PROTECT YOUR STOCK OF PETROL AND YOUR CUSTOMERS' CARS. REMEMBER THAT TRANSPORT AND PETROL WILL BE THE INVADER'S MAIN DIFFICULTIES. MAKE SURE THAT NO INVADER WILL BE ABLE TO GET HOLD OF YOUR CARS, PETROL, MAPS OR BICYCLES.

V

You may be asked by Army and Air Force officers to help in many ways. For instance, the time may come when you will receive orders to block roads or streets in order to prevent the enemy from advancing. Never block a road unless you are told which one you must block. Then you can help by felling trees, wiring them together or blocking the roads with cars. Here, therefore, is the fifth rule :—

(5) BE READY TO HELP THE MILITARY IN ANY WAY. BUT DO NOT BLOCK ROADS UNTIL ORDERED TO DO SO BY THE MILITARY OR L.D.V. AUTHORITIES.

VI

If you are in charge of a factory, store or other works, organise its defence at once. If you are a worker, make sure that you understand the system of defence that has been organised and know what part you have to play in it. Remember always that parachutists and fifth column men are powerless against any organised resistance. They can only succeed if they can create disorganisation. Make certain that no suspicious strangers enter your premises.

You must know in advance who is to take command, who is to be second in command, and how orders are to be transmitted. This chain of command must be built up and you will probably find that ex-officers or N.C.O.'s, who have been in emergencies before, are the best people to undertake such command. The sixth rule is therefore as follows :—

(6) IN FACTORIES AND SHOPS, ALL MANAGERS AND WORKMEN SHOULD ORGANISE SOME SYSTEM NOW BY WHICH A SUDDEN ATTACK CAN BE RESISTED.

VII

The six rules which you have now read give you a general idea of what to do in the event of invasion. More detailed instructions may, when the time comes, be given you by the Military and Police Authorities and by the Local Defence Volunteers; they will NOT be given over the wireless as that might convey information to the enemy. These instructions must be obeyed at once.

Remember always that the best defence of Great Britain is the courage of her men and women. Here is your seventh rule :—

(7) THINK BEFORE YOU ACT. BUT THINK ALWAYS OF YOUR COUNTRY BEFORE YOU THINK OF YOURSELF.

(52194) Wt. / 14,300,000 6/40 Hw.

CHOP SUEY DISHES

4. Special Chop Suey & Rice .. 3.20
5. Beef, Chop Suey & Rice .. 2.90
6. Chicken, Chop Suey & Rice 2.90
7. Pork, Chop Suey & Rice 2.90
8. Prawns, Chop Suey & Rice .. 2.90
9. King Prawns, Chop Suey & Rice 3.40
10. Mushrooms, Chop Suey & Rice 2.70
(Fried Rice 30p extra)

CHOW MEIN DISHES (Noodles)

11. Special Chow Mein 3.50
12. Chicken Chow Mein 3.00
13. Pork Chow Mein 3.00
14. Beef Chow Mein 3.00
15. King Prawn Chow Mein 3.40
16. Prawn Chow Mein 3.00
17. Char Siu Chow Mein 3.00

SATAY DISHES

18. Satay King Prawns & Rice .. 3.50
19. Satay Prawns & Rice 3.20
20. Satay Chicken & Rice 3.20
21. Satay Beef & Rice 3.20
22. Satay Pork & Rice 3.20
(Fried Rice 30p extra)

CURRY DISHES

23. Beef, Curry & Rice 3.00
24. King Prawns, Curry & Rice .. 3.40
25. Prawns, Curry & Rice 3.00
26. Chicken, Curry & Rice 3.00
27. Pork, Curry & Rice 3.00
28. Mushrooms, Curry & Rice .. 2.70
29. Special Curry & Rice 3.20
(Fried Rice 30p extra)

SPECIAL DISHES

30. Special Rice 3.40
31. King Prawns, Pineapple & Rice 3.40
32. Beef, Pineapple & Rice 3.00
33. Roast Chicken & Rice 3.20
34. Chinese Roast Pork & Rice .. 3.20
35. Duck Soo Chow & Rice 3.50
36. Duck, Pineapple & Rice 3.50

"We would not get prosecuted under the Trades Descriptions Act if we included in our advertisement: 'Join Atomic Energy and live a longer life'."

Sir JOHN HILL, Chairman of the United Kingdom Atomic Energy Authority, (UKAEA) 1976.

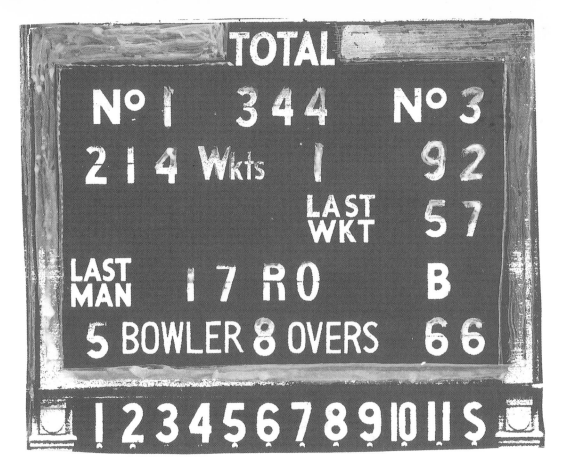

England were unable to match the huge score posted by Gordon Greenidge (No. 1), 214 not out, and the West Indies, in the 2nd Test at Lord's Cricket Ground, London 1984.

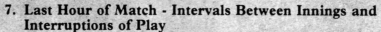

7. Last Hour of Match - Intervals Between Innings and Interruptions of Play

If, at the commencement of the last hour of the match, an interval or interruption of play is in progress or if, during the last hour there is an interval between innings or an interruption of play, the minimum number of overs to be bowled on the resumption of play shall be reduced in proportion to the duration, within the last hour of the match, of any such interval or interruption.

The minimum number of overs to be bowled after a resumption of play shall be calculated as follows:-

(a) In the case of an interval or interruption of play being in progress at the commencement of the last hour of the match, or in the case of a first interval or interruption a deduction shall be made from the minimum of 20 6-ball overs (or 15 8-ball overs).

(b) If there is a later interval or interruption a further deduction shall be made from the minimum number of overs which should have been bowled following the last resumption of play.

(c) These deductions shall be based on the following factors:-

   (i)   the number of overs already bowled in the last hour of the match or, in the case of a later interval or interruption in the last session of play.

   (ii) the number of overs lost as a result of the interval or interruption allowing one 6-ball over for every full three minutes (or one 8-ball over for every full four minutes) of interval or interruption.

   (iii) any over left uncompleted at the end of an innings to be excluded from these calculations.

   (iv) any over left uncompleted at the start of an interruption of play to be completed when play is resumed and to count as one over bowled.

   (v)   an interval to start with the end of an innings and to end 10 minutes later; an interruption to start on the call of 'time' and to end on the call of 'play'.

Alfonso [as if perceiving Ferrando and Gratiano for the first time]—
    Gracious, goodness !
    Am I waking or am I dreaming ?
    Dear old friends and companions !
    You here ?   How so, and why ?   How long ?
    What has brought you ?
    Well, well ! I am delighted !

                    [Aside to Ferrando and Gratiano.]

Alfonso—Come, make haste to the garden,
    Do you hear what that noise is ?
    Who'd have thought it !
    Such harmony ! such voices !
    Such a talented company !
      Who brought it ?
    Come and see, 'twill delight you.

Dorabella—But what is there to see ?

Alfonso—Come, they invite you.

Extract from Cosi Fan Tutte, *by Wolfgang Amadeus Mozart.*

524

A GEORGE III OAK COMMODE-CHAIR, distressed £15-20

525

A VICTORIAN STAINED BEECHWOOD WHEELCHAIR; a Victorian mahogany measuring-stand, the rectangular panelled base with upright and brass arm (2) £50-80

526

A PAIR OF WICKER GARDEN CHAIRS; and two Victorian chairs, distressed (4) £20-30

527

A MID-VICTORIAN GRAINED NURSING CHAIR with cartouche shaped metal-framed back, lacking upholstery, on turned legs; and a late Victorian upholstered centre table with two tiers on splayed legs, 32in. (81.5cm.) wide (2) £50-100

528

AN EARLY VICTORIAN BEECHWOOD INVALID'S CHAIR with rectangular padded back, arm-rests and seat on turned tapering legs with carrying-handles to the front and back £40-60

529

A MID-VICTORIAN BEECHWOOD ARMCHAIR with twisted railed back and sides, the seat previously caned on turned splayed legs £60-80

530

A STAINED PINE FOLDING BENCH 50½in. (128cm.) wide £15-30

531

A LATE VICTORIAN MAHOGANY DESK TUB CHAIR with U-shaped padded back and seat covered in brown leather on a revolving cruciform base £20-30

532

A SET OF FOUR BEECHWOOD FOLDING GARDEN CHAIRS with striped upholstery (4) £20-40

533

ANOTHER SET OF FOUR (4) £20-40

534

ANOTHER SET OF FOUR   (4)
                                                   £20-40

535

A SET OF THREE, similar, with plain buff-coloured
upholstery; a beechwood deck chair; and a metal deck chair
                                                       (5)
                                                   £20-40

536

A PAIR OF MID-VICTORIAN WALNUT SOFAS, each of rounded
rectangular shape with arched padded back and seat
covered in black buttoned canvas, one end divided off with
an arm, on a plinth base
102in. (259cm.) wide   (2)
                                                 £100-200

537

AN EARLY VICTORIAN MAHOGANY HALF-TESTER BED-CANOPY;
and quantity of other bed ends, etc.   (a lot)
                                                  £50-100

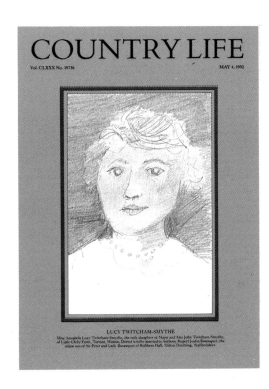

COUNTRY LIFE

Vol. CLXXX No. 19736   MAY 4, 1992

LUCY TWITCHAM-SMYTHE

Miss Annabels Lucy Twitcham-Smythe, the only daughter of Major and Mrs John Twitcham-Smythe, of Little Glebe Farm, Tarrant, Hinton, Dorset is to be married to Anthony Rupert Justin Bosanquet, the oldest son of Sir Peter and Lady Bosanquet of Rubbers Hall, Milton Dinchling, Staffordshire.

Major and Mrs Henry Twitcham-Smythe
request the pleasure of
your company at the marriage
of their daughter
Lucy
to
Mr Anthony Rupert Justin Bosanquet
on Saturday 9th May 1992
at 3 o'clock
at St Peter's Church, Tarrant
and afterwards at
Little Glebe Farm, Tarrant

R.S.V.P.
Little Glebe Farm
Tarrant
Hinton
Dorset

"We didn't see anybody in the park we liked better than ourselves."

Extract from Nanny Says *by Sir Hugh Casson and Joyce Grenfell.*

The Princess of Wales, and all the princesses of the blood royal, should be addressed as "Ma'am" by the aristocracy and gentry, and as "Your Royal Highness" by all other classes. The wives of the princes of the blood royal should also be addressed as "Ma'am" by the aristocracy and gentry, and as "Your Royal Highness" by all other classes.

A foreign prince bearing the title of serene highness should be addressed as "Prince," and not as "Sir," by the aristocracy and gentry, and as "Your Serene Highness" by all other classes.

A foreign princess, also bearing the title of serene highness, should be styled "Princess" when addressed colloquially by the upper classes, but not as "Ma'am," as in the case of the Royal Family of England, and as "Your Serene Highness" by all other classes.

An English duke should be addressed as "Duke" by the aristocracy and gentry, and not as "Your Grace" by members of either of these classes. All other classes should address him colloquially as "Your Grace."

An English duchess should be addressed as "Duchess" by all persons conversing with her belonging to the upper classes, and as "Your Grace" by all other classes.

A marquis, colloquially, should be addressed as "Lord A."

A marchioness should be addressed as "Lady A." by the upper classes. It would be a mistake to address an English marquis as "Marquis," or a marchioness as "Marchioness," colloquially speaking. All other classes should address them either as "My Lord" or "Your Lordship," "My Lady" or "Your Ladyship."

Extract from the Manners and Rules of Good Society by A Member of the Aristocracy, 1887.

Tis a fine opening day!
To the moors will away
all the World and his wife and his kin,
over bents, hags and bogs,
with drivers and dogs
keen as Coleman's best brand to begin.
Every butt with new turfs is OK,
fingers itch to be blazing away.
With the grouse in the ling
wild and strong on the wing,
we must all go a-shooting today!

W. Carter Platts, 1905

Romantic Bradford weekend

Friday evening

Arrive at your hotel and settle in before champagne dinner for two at the Leeming Wells Country Hotel, Oxenhope. Take a nostalgic steam railway trip through the beautiful Worth Valley between Keighley and Haworth. Stroll down cobbled Main Street browsing around the art galleries and on to the Bronte Parsonage - home of the famous literary family.

Saturday

Head out to the heather covered moors which inspired Emily's passionate novel 'Wuthering Heights' - and then savour the delights of a gourmet picnic surrounded by fantastic panoramic views.

Afternoon tea at East Riddlesden Hall in the Great Barn and see this wonderful example of a 17th Century Manor House.

Evening

Spend the night watching top class drama or listening to a classical concert at St Georges Hall. Order room service back at your hotel and 'cuddle' the night away.

Sunday Morning

To Saltaire village. Stroll down the canal watching the barges slowly drifting along and amble up to the Bingley Five Rise Locks. Take the Waterbus back to Saltaire and view the 1853 Gallery in Salts Mill.
Find yourself a cosy moorland inn for lunch and settle down to traditional Yorkshire fayre.

Extract from Bradford, a Travel Guide, 1992 *listing local attractions with weekend breaks.*

Rule   Brit - an - nia.   Brit - an - nia rule the waves;

Repeat in Chorus.

Britons nev - er, nev - er, nev - er : will be slaves! :

Britons nev - er, nev - er, nev - er : will be slaves! :

<u>OUTDOOR DUTY AND INDOOR PATROL DUTY</u> (lunchtime)

The member of staff and sixth formers on duty should patrol both
the grounds and indoors of the school. Please meet all the girls
on duty outside the staffroom at the beginning of the duty period.
Liaise closely with girls on duty and decide who will cover the
various areas. It is suggested that the member of staff should
alternate between outdoor and indoor duty on a weekly basis.
(i) Indoor Patrol Duty - as for morning break above. Girls should be
    sent outside at lunchtime in the Autumn and Summer terms, weather
    permitting.
(ii) Outdoor Duty - If wet, go to the library to supervise behaviour.
If fine, ensure that the girls remain 'within bounds' - see school
rules and note that the bounds on the north side of the field are indicated
by the touch line of the Boys' Prep. Department football pitch. Girls
may only visit the Boys' School at lunch-time if attending an organised
activity or if they have a note signed by a Deputy Head Mistress.
Please check carefully any girls going into the Boys' School grounds.
Ask what activity they are attending and take a note of their names
and the activity concerned.
Girls and boys may meet at the gate between the two schools, but should
not go beyond it. They <u>may not</u> meet on the boundary between their Prep.
football pitch and our field. The guideline for behaviour agreed between
Mrs. Girton and the Head Master is that <u>there should be no physical</u>
<u>contact between boys and girls during the school day.</u> Holding hands
is not allowed. Please enforce this rule. Staff on duty please enter
the Boys' School grounds by the gate and check that no girl is loitering
near the shubbery (to the left of the cricket pitch). Boys should not
be in our grounds and should only be within our buildings if they have
a good reason (eg. an organised activity) - take the names of any
suspicious 'visitors'. Discourage silly or dangerous behaviour and
check that litter is put in the bins. Find out which sixth formers are on
outdoor duty and work as a team. Visit the lake and take the name of
anyone found there.
Note: The second member of staff scheduled for this duty (initials in
brackets) is asked to stand by if needed or to cover for absence.

<u>DINING ROOM DUTY</u> (lunchtime) Please see Miss Klondike who will explain
what is involved.

<u>PREP. SUPERVISION</u> - See separate notice.

<u>LATE DUTY</u> (after school) - See separate notice.

<u>LATE DUTY</u> (during assembly)

Collect the 'late book' from the staffroom and be in the late room
(room 25) from 9 a.m. until the end of main assembly. Anyone arriving
during this time should first sign-in (check that she has done so),
signing-in sheets are outside Mrs Gammer's office, then present herself
at the late room where she should wait until assembly has ended. Ask the
reason for lateness, note her name and reason and report any suspicious
excuses to the appropriate teacher.

RADLETT HALL
PREPARATORY
SCHOOL FOR BOYS

"Upon the education of the people of this country the fate of this country depends."

Benjamin Disraeli

From a speech to the House of Commons, 15 June 1874.

PASTIME WITH GOOD COMPANY
KING HENRY VIII (1491-1547)

Pastime with good company I love,
and shall until I die.
Grudge who will but none deny
So God be pleas'd thus live will I.
For my pastance,
Hunt, sing and dance,
My heart is set.
All goodly sport.
For my comfort who shall me let?

Youth must have some daliance,
Of good or ill some pastance.
Company me thinks the best,
All thoughts and fancies to digest
For idleness, Is chief mistress.
Of vices all.
Then who can say
But mirth and play
Is best of all?

"We pledge to work together, in the spirit of mutual trust and through selfless devot

our jobs, for continuous improvement of corporate and personal performances."

Extract from Quest for Prosperity, The Life of a Japanese Industrialist, *by Konosuke Matsushita.*

Form of Declaration of Result

PARLIAMENTARY ELECTION - 9TH JUNE 1983

CONSTITUENCY OF FINCHLEY

The percentage of electors voting at the Election for the

Constituency of Finchley was .....79..37..%

I, JOHN CHARLIE TIPLADY, Returning Officer for the Constituency

of Finchley, hereby declare that the total number of votes

given for each Candidate at the Election was as follows:-

MARY HELEN ANSCOMB (RAIL-NOT MOTORWAY INDEPENDENT) .....42.

MARGARET JANE JOACHIM (LIBERAL-SDP ALLIANCE)   ....7763....

ANTHONY JOSEPH NOONAN (BAN EVERY LICENSING LAW   75
                       SOCIETY CANDIDATE)   ....

LAURENCE GREGORY SPIGEL (THE LABOUR PARTY   10302
                         CANDIDATE)   ....

LORD DAVID EDWARD SUTCH (OFFICIAL MONSTER RAVING   235
                         LOONY PARTY CANDIDATE)...........

~~MARGARET THATCHER (CONSERVATIVE PARTY)~~

MARGARET HILDA THATCHER (THE CONSERVATIVE PARTY   19616
                         CANDIDATE)   ....

BRIAN CLIFFORD WAREHAM (PARTY OF ASSOCIATES WITH   27
                        LICENSEES)   ....

DAVID ALEC WEBB (ANTI-CENSORSHIP/REFORM OF   28
                 OBSCENE PUBLICATIONS ACTS)   ....

BENJAMIN COLLINGHAM WEDMORE (BELGRANO BLOOD?   13
                             HUNGER)   ....

ANTHONY PETER WHITEHEAD (LAW AND ORDER IN GOTHAM   37
                         CITY)   ....

SIMONE JOAN WILKINSON (WOMEN-LIFE ON EARTH/   277
                       ECOLOGY PARTY)   ....

and that the said ....MARGARET HILDA THATCHER....... has been

duly elected to serve as a Member of Parliament for the said

Constituency.

QUESTIONS FOR ORAL ANSWER—*continued*

Questions to the Prime Minister will start at 3.15 p.m.

★Q1　**Mr Andrew MacKay** (East Berkshire):　To ask the Prime Minister, if he will list his official engagements for Tuesday 11th February.

★Q2　**Mr Andy Stewart** (Sherwood):　To ask the Prime Minister, if he will list his official engagements for Tuesday 11th February.

★Q3　**Mr James Hill** (Southampton, Test):　To ask the Prime Minister, if he will visit the City and Port of Southampton.

★Q4　**Mr Jack Thompson** (Wansbeck):　To ask the Prime Minister, if he will list his official engagements for Tuesday 11th February.

★Q5　**Mr Ian Taylor** (Esher):　To ask the Prime Minister, if he will list his official engagements for Tuesday 11th February.

★Q6　**Sir Anthony Grant** (South West Cambridgeshire):　To ask the Prime Minister, if he will list his official engagements for Tuesday 11th February.

★Q7　**Mr Eric Martlew** (Carlisle):　To ask the Prime Minister, if he will list his official engagements for Tuesday 11th February.

★Q8　**Mr Bruce Grocott** (The Wrekin):　To ask the Prime Minister, if he will list his official engagements for Tuesday 11th February.

★Q9　**Mrs Irene Adams** (Paisley North):　To ask the Prime Minister, if he will list his official engagements for Tuesday 11th February.

OBITUARY

HOUSE OF LORDS
The following Members have died this year

Reginald Alfred Wells-Pestell, Lord Wells-Pestell (*died* 17 1 91)
James Victor Broke Saumarez, Lord de Saumarez (*died* 20 1 91)
Rhys Gerran Lloyd, Lord Lloyd of Kilgerran (*died* 30 1 91)
George William Anthony Tufton, Lord Hothfield (*died* 5 2 91)
James Hans Hamilton, Lord Holm Patrick (*died* 15 2 91)
Clement Napier Bertram Mitford, Lord Redesdale (*died* 3 3 91)
William George Penney, Lord Penney (*died* 3 3 91)
Donald Kaberry, Lord Kaberry of Adel (*died* 13 3 91)
John Edward Pelham, Earl of Yarborough (*died* 15 3 91)
George Rowland Stanley Baring, Earl of Cromer (*died* 16 3 91)

William Philip Sidney, Viscount De L'Isle (*died* 5 4 91)
Richard Francis Roger Yarde Butler, Lord Churston (*died* 9 4 91)
Harry Bernard Taylor, Lord Taylor of Mansfield (*died* 11 4 91)
Rowland Roberts Blades, Lord Ebbisham (*died* 12 4 91)
Henry David Leonard George Walston, Lord Walston (*died* 29 5 91)
Jestyn Reginald Austen Plantagenet Philips, Viscount St Davids (*died* 10 6 91)
Alexander Francis St Vincent Baring, Lord Ashburton (*died* 14 6 91)
Bernard James Miles, Lord Miles (*died* 14 6 91)
Anthony Crespigny Claud Vivian, Lord Vivian (*died* 24 6 91)
Spencer Douglas Loch, Lord Loch (*died* 24 6 91)
George Fielden MacLeod, Lord MacLeod of Fuinary (*died* 27 6 91)
George William Lawes Jackson, Lord Allerton (*died* 1 7 91)
Martin Richard Attlee, Earl Attlee (*died* 27 7 91)
John Desmond Cavendish Brownlow, Lord Lurgan (*died* 17 9 91)
Elaine Frances Burton, Baroness Burton of Coventry (*died* 6 10 91)
Arthur Hugh Elsdale Molson, Lord Molson (*died* 13 10 91)

ROLL OF HONOUR.

580 CASUALTIES TO OFFICERS.

143 REPORTED DEAD.

Reported by the War Office u.
...s:—

KILLED.

ABBEY, Sec. Lieut. C. G., Oxford and Bucks L..
AUSTIN, Sec. Lieut. G. F., Cheshire Regt.
BAGSHAWE, Capt. E. G. C., Yorkshire Regt.
BENNETT, Sec. Lieut. S. G., Suffolk Regt.
BLAIR, Capt. R. C. R., D.S.O., Border Regt.
BLAKE, Capt. G. P. R. Welsh Fusiliers.
CALDER, Sec. Lieut. A. F., Argyll and Sutherland
CASSELS, Lieut. F. L., Royal Engineers.
CHALKER, Lieut. E., Royal Field Artillery.
CHARD, Capt. R. A. F., Royal Fusiliers.
CONGREVE, Major W. La T., D.S.O., Rifle Brigade.
COOK, Sec. Lieut. A. B. K., Royal Fusiliers.
KITE, Lieut. C. E. V., Sherwood Foresters.
CRICHTON, Lieut. J. F., The Black Watch.
EMPSON, Sec. Lieut. R. A. F., King's R. Rifle C
Machine Gun Corps.
FEATHERSTONHAUGH, Capt. H., Royal Fusiliers
FOULKES-WINKS, Sec. Lieut. O. W., Middlesex
Trench Mortar Batty.
FRANKLIN, Capt. H., Royal Fusiliers.
GODFREY, Sec. Lieut. L. G., Royal Welsh Fusiliers.
GOLD, Sec. Lieut. P., Scots Guards.
GORDON, Lieut. H. B., Royal Sussex Regiment.
GOSLING, Capt. F. W., Manchester Regiment.
GRIMMOND, Sec. Lieut. A., Royal Scots.
GUNSON, Lieut. L. R. S., Royal Garrison Artillery.
HAMMOND-CHAMBERS, Capt. H. B. B., Royal Lancaster 1
HAYDON, Sec. Lieut. E. F. B., Royal Field Artillery.
HYLAND, Sec. Lieut. H. B., Machine Gun Corps.
JAMESON, Sec. Lieut. A. B., Cambridgeshire Regiment.
JOHNSON, Sec. Lieut. S., Suffolk Regiment.
KEMBLE, Lieut. H. N., Suffolk Regiment.
KENNEFICK, Capt. E. H., Essex Regiment.
LADELL, Lieut. J. F., Middlesex Regiment.
LEWIS, Capt. G. S., Middlesex Regiment.
LYONS, Capt. W. T., Royal Lancaster Regiment.
MACNICOL, Sec. Lieut. H. M., Norfolk Regiment.
MADDER, Sec. Lieut. A., Gloucester Regt., attd. Machine
Corps.
MANSON, Sec. Lieut. J. C., Royal Fusiliers.
MAY, Capt. R. T., Royal Sussex Regiment
MILLAR, Sec. Lieut. L., Durham Light Infantry.
MORGAN, Sec. Lieut. W. C., Norfolk Regiment.
MURRAY, Lieut. H. B., Argyll and Sutherland Highlanders.
PAGE, Sec. Lieut. H., Royal Welsh Fusiliers.
PEACOCK, Sec. Lieut. E. G., Royal Fusiliers.
PHILLIPS, Capt. Hon. R. E., Royal Fusiliers.
PLATTS, Lieut. A. L., Suffolk Regiment.
PROCTER, Sec. Lieut. A. D. G., Royal Fusiliers.
ROBERTS, Sec. Lieut. D. C., South Wales Borderers.
ROBINSON, Sec. Lieut. A. A., Royal Garrison Artillery.
ROTHBAND, Capt. J. E., Manchester Regiment.
SANDERSON, Sec. Lieut. G. S., London Regiment.
SCALF, Capt. G. D., Royal Welsh Fusiliers.
SIMMS, Capt. W., Royal Warwickshire Regiment.
STREET, Lieut. F., Royal Fusiliers.
STONE, Sec. Lieut. D., Royal Warwickshire Regiment.
TABER, Sec. Lieut. S. J. H., Essex Regiment.
THOMSON, Capt. A. M., R.A.M.C., attd. R. Sussex Regiment.
THOMSON, Sec. Lieut. K. D., Argyll and Sutherland Highlanders.
TINLEY, Sec. Lieut. J., Royal Scots Fusiliers.
TRIMMER, Sec. Lieut. W. C., Oxford and Bucks Light Infantry.
VAUGHAN, Capt. G. C., Devonshire Regiment.
VOELCKER, Sec. Lieut. H. E., South Lancashire Regiment.
WAREHAM, Sec. Lieut. L. J., Worcestershire Regiment.
WELLER, Qrmr. and Hon. Lieut. W. R., Argyll and Sutherland
Highrs.
WILLIAMS, Sec. Lieut. L. A., Duke of Cornwall's Light Infantry.
WILLIAMS-VAUGHAN, Sec. Lieut. J. C. A., S. Wales Bordrs., attd.
Machine Gun Corps.
WYLLIE, Maj. W. T., Durham Light Infantry.

DIED OF WOUNDS.

FRENCH, Sec. Lieut. P. V., Durham Light Infantry.

WOUNDED.

ABBOTTS, Sec. Lieut. R. W., Machine Gun Corps.
ALEXANDER, Capt. W. S., Cameronians.
ALLAN, Sec. Lieut. H. D., Argyll and Sutherland Highlanders.
ALLAN, Sec. Lieut. W. D., Royal Sussex Regiment.
ALLEN, Lieut. V. C., Royal Field Artillery.

LAMBART, Capt. E. O. C., R. Berks Regt., attd. Trench Mortar
Batt.
LANDON, Sec. Lieut. W. H. P., Royal Field Artillery.
LARHAM, Sec. Lieut. P. E., Royal Fusiliers.
LAWRENCE, Capt. L. G., Worcestershire Regiment.
LAWSON, Capt. R., Royal Army Medical Corps.
LEWIS, Sec. Lieut. T. D., Royal Lancaster Regiment.
LLEWHELLIN, Sec. Lieut. G. E., Norfolk Regiment.
LOUGH, Sec. Lieut. C. T., Worcestershire Regiment.
LUCAS, Capt. R. H., R.A.M.C., attd. R. Fusiliers.
LUCK, Lieut. C. C. J., Seaforth Highlanders.
MACAULEY, Sec. Lieut. W., Royal Welsh Fusiliers.
McCLENAGHAN, Lieut. G. M., Royal West Kent Regiment.
McCRIRICK, Sec. Lieut. C. S., Black Watch
McFARLANE, Sec. Lieut. J. ...
MACFARLAN...

Royal Sussex Regiment.

... Lieut. A., Middlesex Regiment.
..., Sec. Lieut. W. E., Durham Light Infantry.
...INHOLD, Sec. Lieut. W. J., Royal Engineers.
RICH, Sec. Lieut. M. D., Royal Warwickshire Regiment.
RICHARDSON, Sec. Lieut. G., Devonshire Regiment.
RIPPON, Sec. Lieut. A. E. S., Royal Fusiliers.
RODGERS, Capt. R. W. C. M., Royal Garrison Artillery.
ROBINS, Sec. Lieut. H., King's Royal Rifle Corps.
ROWLEY, Sec. Lieut. R. F., Royal Field Artillery.
RUDDELL, Capt. E. E., Royal Scots.
RUSHWORTH, Sec. Lieut. F. A., Yorkshire Regiment
RUSSELL, Sec. Lieut. R. P., Royal ...
SADLER, Sec. Lieut. H. ...
ST. P...

... Royal Scots.
... Durham Light Infantry.
..., D.S.O., Loyal North Lancashire Regiment.
..., Sec. Lieut. A. A., Royal Fusiliers.
...ACKE, Sec. Lieut. E. H., Machine Gun Corps.
VAILE, Sec. Lieut. P. A., London Regiment.
VAN-MILLINGEN, Sec. Lieut. C. A. M., Rifle Brigade.
WADE, Capt. M. C., Royal Warwickshire Regiment.
WALDRON, Sec. Lieut. R., Royal Field Artillery.
WALKER, Sec. Lieut. G. R. S., West Yorkshire Regiment.
WALKER, Lieut. R. H., Seaforth Highlanders.
WALTER, Capt. J. W., Durham Light Infantry.
WATKINS, Sec. Lieut. A. G. W., Royal Warwickshire Regiment.
WATTS, Sec. Lieut. L. M., Royal Engineers.

SECOND LIST.

KILLED.

ALGIE, Capt. C., New Zealand Infantry.
BLACK, Sec. Lieut. A. M., Cameron Highlanders.
BONE, Sec. Lieut. J. H., Sherwood Foresters.
BOUCHER, Sec. Lieut. B. R., East Yorkshire Regiment.
BRAITHWAITE, Sec. Lieut. J. L., Royal Horse Artillery.
CROSS, Sec. Lieut. W., Leicestershire Regiment.
DAWSON, Sec. Lieut. H. H. M., Royal Field Artillery.
GILSON, ...
... Regiment.
...eron Highlanders.
... Black Watch.
...North Lancashire Regime
...en. E. C., C.B., D.S.O.
... Welsh Fusiliers.
...rkshire Regiment.
... Gun Corps.
...ian Mounted Rifles.
...al Horse Artillery.
...on Highlanders.
...k Watch.
...Regiment.
...ron Highldrs., attd. Lo
...orcestershire Regimen
...herwood Foresters.
...oyal Flying Corps.
... Royal Scots Fusilie
... Sutherland Highla
...ine Gun Corps.
...Yorkshire Regimen
...ster Regt., attd. Ma
..., now reported Kill
...umberland Fusilie
... Killed, now reporte
...Yorkshire Regime
...now reported Kille
...
...UNDS.
...S.O., Royal Fusil
...affordshire Regim
... Regiment.
...ssex Regiment.
...est Kent Regim
...ddlesex Regimen
...egiment.
...al Inniskilling Fusiliers.
... E., Royal Warwickshire Reg
... West Yorkshire Regiment.
...eut. R. E., Gloucestershire Regim
...W. F. C., R. W. Surrey Regt., attd. R.
...ON, Lieut. A. S., Canadian Infantry.
...S., Lieut. H. E., Machine Gun Corps.
SAMUEL, Sec. Lieut. G. S., East Yorkshire Regiment
STRIBLING, Lieut. F. G., Sherwood Foresters.
TOMLINSON, Sec. Lieut. R. H., Liverpool Regiment
WOLSELEY, Lieut. W. B., Royal Field Artillery.
WREFORD-BROWN, Capt. O. E., Northumberland

WOUNDED.

ADAM, Sec. Lieut. R. G. S., Royal Field Artillery.
ADDIS, Sec. Lieut. T. H. L., Royal ... Fusiliers.
ADDISON, Sec. Lieut. ... ders.
A... ... ottish Bord
... ordrs., att
... landers.
... ment.
... attd. Ma
... ield Artillery.
...ameron Highlanders.
...o., A., Royal Welsh Fusiliers.
...w., Leicestershire Regiment.
... Lieut. W., Argyll and Sutherland High
... Lieut. E., Gordon Highlanders.
...RON, Sec. Lieut. A. D., Cameron Highlanders.
CAMPBELL, Sec. Lieut. S. C., Cameron Highlanders, at
Mortar Battery.
CARPENTER, Sec. Lieut. A. E., R.W. Kent Regt., att
Gun Corps.
COX, Sec. Lieut. J. P., Manchester Regt.attd. Trench M
CROGGAN, Capt. J. F. S., Sherwood Foresters.
CUTHBERT, Sec. Lieut. J. G. G., Machine Gun Corps.
DARLING, Sec. Lieut. J. A., King's Own Scottish Bord
DAVIES, Sec. Lieut. D. H. S., R. Warwick Regt. and
Corps.
DEANS, Sec. Lieut. J., Cameronians, attd. Trench Mor
DEVIS, Sec. Lieut. F., Royal Warwickshire Regiment.
DUKE, Sec. Lieut. L., York and Lancaster Regiment.
DUNBAR, Sec. Lieut. W. P., Black Watch.
DUNCAN WALLACE, Sec. Lieut. A. M., Black Watch.
DURNFORD, Sec. Lieut. B., Royal Fusiliers.
DURRANT, Sec. Lieut. K. G., Gloucestershire Regimen
ELVERY, Sec. Lieut. W. M. M., Royal Inniskilling Fus
ENGLAND, Lieut. W. F., Liverpool Regt., attd. Lanc
FINDLEY, Lieut. T. L., Canadian Trench Mortar Batt
FORD, Capt. G. R., North Staffordshire Regiment.
FORSTER, Sec. Lieut. ... Welsh Regiment.

MONDAY, JULY 3, 1916.

FORWARD IN THE WEST.

FIERCE BATTLES ON THE SOMME.

Thanks to the very complete and effective artillery preparation, thanks also to the dash of our infantry, our losses have been very slight,

GOOD NEW...

727 R.; Reed, 585 G. E.; Richardson, 254 G.; Robinson, Sgt.-Maj. J. L.; Ruane, 1266 Sgt. P.; Rutter, 733 T. 1102 M.; Stobart, 1132 J.; Tait, 1052 L.-Cpl. J. C.; 2212 A. E.; Thompson, 1 R.; Turnbull, 1547 H. 088 Cpl. T. D.; Wallace, 191 W.; Wardhaugh, 885 S. k, 419 J.; Watkin, 79 T.; Welsh, 835 W.; White, ; Young, 1092 L.-Cpl. E.

WICK R.—Daniel, 17118 G.; Davis, 2342 L.-Cpl. J.; 6798 W. L.; Gale, 6075 G. W.; Gardener, 3553 A. 3864 H.; Mead, 4743 G.; Tew, 16764 C. H.

Aldridge, 7501 E. J.; Bates, 20423 T.; Baxter, 12212 owell, 7789 T.; Bird, 19100 L.-Cpl. A.; Boreham, 18663 riggs, 7472 L.-Cpl. H.; Buckingham, 18003 L.; Bundy, L.-Cpl. C. E.; Bushnell, 7514 A.; Chandler, 1284 J. W.; 1396 J.; Denham, 7284 W. E.; Dilley, 7550 A. A.; 8107 L.-Cpl. H.; Eldridge, 15619 A.; Fletcher, 21187 eeman, 7573 L.-Sgt. C. A.; Graddon, 3032 V. H.; Groves, Hall, 8130 J. H.; Harrington, 2215 J.; Hill, 8136 ill, 10371 T.; Holt, 11983 A. S.; Honeywood, 7594 H.; od, 10399 T.; Hughes, 8145 L.-Cpl. T. W.; Hutchins, Jackson, 7068 A.; Kilby, 3549 A. F.; Kitson, 20973 Langston, 9234 W.; Longbottom, 9432 A. B.; Long- 620 Cpl. W. E.; Ludgate, 8432 Cpl. J. H.; Manning, R.; May, 2265 J.; Mess, 19202 V. A.; Mills, 7949 A.; 19101 J.; O'Rourke, 7918 M.; Pilling, 8191 E.; Pritchard, Pursglove, 18656 G.; Rance, 20816 W. C.; Smith, T. S.; Staines, 7678 L.-Cpl. W.; Stickston, 3271 S. J.; ell, 7973 W. G.; Taylor, 916 W. H.; Thom, 7431 L.-Cpl. Tolley, 17533 E.; Western, 7062 L.-Cpl. C. J.; ky, 18000 A. W.; Wood, 7981 Sgt. A. W.

ATTD. BUFFS (E. KENT R.).—Breadon, 8666 W.; Bowe, L.; Johnson, 7561 H. P.; May, 3008 R.; Read, 8556 Thain, 8076 E. J. B.; Winterbottom, 7511 A. R.; Gowing, 6949 G.

—Jeffery, 9264 W.; Stobe, 15492 J. B.

R.—Aldridge, 7944 L.-Cpl. R.; Allen, 15592 E.; Bailey, Cpl. C.; Bailey, 13281 G.; Baker, 9366 E. G.; Bennett, gt. J. J.; Benton, 14422 H.; Boreham, 12063 A. W.; 8104 L.-Cpl. C.; Borrett, 13181 H.; Brown, 7244 E.; c, 19202 F.; Bunten, 15872 F. R.; Bush, 12585 H. V.; an, 15074 F. E.; Chenery, 12173 J. W.; Chippendale, A.; Clarke, 12356 S. H.; Crick, 12145 L.-Cpl. H. J.; 20008 J.; Dare, 6121 H.; Day, 12229 A.; Day, 15731 Drake, 19416 W.; Flack, 10238 Sgt. E.; Fogg, 8461 E. G.; Foreman, 9085 T.; Fuller, 8644 E. W.; Gardner, E. J.; Gatward, 8629 R. W.; Girling, 12397 H. G.; Good- 8548 L.-Cpl. C. E.; Griggs, 12104 W.; Hammond, 12948 urst, 14624 E.; Jacobs, 18439 W.; King, 22319 A.; 2305 L.-Cpl. A. S.; Eingard, 12596 A.; Long, 18615 W. J.; ll, 22383 W. A.; Mole, 9124 Cpl. E.; Mufet, 17505 J.; 23798 W.; Pannell, 8480 L.-Cpl. W.; Potter, 19229 G.; 8932 L.-Sgt. H.; Powell, 8987 R.; Raymond, 12341 C.; 9242 L.-Cpl. H.; Saunders, 12334 S.; Seaman, 13160 G. W.; Sebborn, 14958 A. H.; Sharman, 18680 J.; 7823 W.; Simpson, 18817 L.-Cpl. A. A.; Smith, 12999 E. mith, 18942 W.; Sneesby, 12202 G.; Sore, 12211 L.-Cpl. Parkes, 20220 E.; Steward, 18180 D.; Stubbens, 12560 ylor, 23748 E.; Taylor, 9482 R.; Twinn, 18174 A.; 7273 Sgt. E.; Watson, 9207 J.; Wilkins, 18125 R.; ns, 9281 H. H.; Woolston, 12955 L.-Cpl. W.

L.I.—Beckett, 8722 Cpl. R. C.; Bristow, 17061 Cpl. Dormand, 15789 T.; Lintern, 16894 W.; Lock, 17343 Moore, 20433 F. G.; Parsons, 10377 F.; Pearson, 16795 T.; Shopland, 20728 F.

S R.—Acton, 9444 C.; Adams, 1158 N.; Addy, 289 E.; 24456 J.; Alderthay, 12370 D.; Allatt, 248 T. H.; Amys, Arbuckle, 11107 R.; Ashton, 9531 L.-Cpl. H.; Atkin- 187 H.; Atkinson, 17669 L.-Cpl. J.; Bagnall, 8998 Sgt. J.; 8910 F.; Balls, 9232 W.; Bamborough, 8886 J.; Ban- 58 L.-Cpl. G.; Bardy, 17205 H.; Barrass, 24480 T.; 5606 Sgt. H. G.; Barter, 8288 L.-Sgt. H.; Barton, 7748 eman, 104 Cpl. P.; Bell, 17103 C. H.; Bell, 8292 L.-Cpl. ts, 7656 L.-Cpl. C.; Benmann, 7795 E.; Birch, 8436 ackburn, 24418 B. M.; Blackwell, 12421 W. oomfield, 9219 L.-Cpl. R.; Bloomfield, 8626 L.-Cpl. T.; 8799 Cpl. W.; Brack, 7462 K.; Bradley, 17240 B.; 8786 G.; Brannan, 17170 T.; Brannen, 7991 J.; 8683 J. H.; Brooker, 9170 L.-Cpl. M.; Brown, 8162 own, 7629 L.-Cpl. J.; Brown, 9545 T.; Brummitt, 8252 unton, 24028 W. H.; Buckham, 9340 R.; Burke, 7607 nett, 8441 L.-Sgt. T.; Burns, 7375 F.; Bush, 11560 A.; 9184 Sgt. B.; Buxton, 22683 J.; Caller, 8697 Cpl. J.; 211 H. B.; Carter, 1074 D. F.; Cassidy, 10337 Cpl. J.; 8401 L.-Cpl. C.; Chapman, 23311 E.; Chapman, 22184 arlton, 8751 F.; Charville, 9336 L.-Cpl. E.; Chaytor, Cheshire, 7938 F.; Churn, 9767 Dmr. W.; Clark, A.; Clarke, 9589 R.; Clark, 8704 W.; Clayton, 9414 Cliffe, 7724 S.; Clover, 18327 Cpl. F.; Coates, 1567 Cobb, 8328 A.; Coldwell, 22142 C.; Collett, 23608 E.; 7532 L.-Cpl. G.; Coltman, 7945 E.; Conlan, 10181 V.; Cooper, 8439 J.; Cooper, 21472 W.; Cooper, 23620 oper, 9247 Sgt. W. J.; Cox, 8904 J.; Craven, 8354 H.; w, 17746 T.; Crossfield, 21622 W.; Crossland, 24428 ssland, 1405 H.; Crumley, 10009 J.; Cullingford, 781 nningham, 5164 Co. Sgt.-Maj. J.; Curtis, 9183 A.; 5785 L.-Cpl. J.; Dayes, 11728 G.; Deehan, 9526 F.; 19306 J.; Dent, 11723 L.-Cpl. T.; Dove, 8489 L.; Dodgson, 12083 L.; Dolan, 9173 A.; Drake, 17745 D. G.; Draper, 15509 W. C. B.; Drinkwater, 24003 Ellison, 9229 F.; Emmett, 8567 R.; Essim, 24353 A.; 056 L.-Cpl. J.; Farmer, 10416 A.; Farrand, 9796 H.; 8351 Cpl. L.; Farrel, 7210 Cpl. J.; Farthing, 9329 L.; Fearnley, 13303 A.; Fenton, 8305 G.; Fettes, 8581 G.; 31 J.; Fish, 17663 A.; Fish, 21585 J.; Fitzpatrick, Foley, 8360 Cpl. F.; Foot, 7452 W.; Forster, 17222 oster, 8620 C.; Freeman, 9022 H.; Fuguel, R.; Galley, 17124 A.; Galloway, 24453 H.; 24429 T.; Gibb, 24184 R. —; Gibson, 8543 ss, 9125 G.; Goodhall, 8837 W.; Gray, 8486 C.; 624 T.; Gregory, 8922 Sgt. E.; Gregory, 10057 H.; 8896 L.-Cpl. F.; Haines, 8208 A.; Halifax, 8518 J.; 84 H.; Hall, 18584 J.; Hall, 13084 J. W.; Hallam, Hannibal, 8599 H.; Hardcastle, 9280 J.; Harding, A. L.; Harvey, 9195 L.-Cpl. J.; Hayward, 8398 L.; 558 H.; Hilcoat, 8593 R.; Hirst, 572 L.-Cpl. F.; 15 J.; Hoitt, 8616 Sgt. S.; Holcroft, 1081 E.; Holmes, Holmes, 9542 R.; Holmes, 19758 L.-Cpl. W.; Hern, Howard, 510 H.; Howes, 8765 J.; Howe 9046 C.; Howson, 1425 H.; Hudson, 350 Sgt. A.; Hudson, Hughes 9309 P.; Hulbert 7865 W.; Hurdle

DORSET. R., ATTD. HAMPS. R.—Dunent, 10275 G.; Dyke, 13217 C. E.; Pike, 11045 H. F.; Willis, 10861 Act.-Cpl. W. J.

DORSET. R., ATTD. WILTS. R.—Jackson, 7435 J. W.

BLACK WATCH.—Freestone, 13060 S.; Gallacher, 2197 A.; Gallacher, 4853 W.; Lister, 1026 R.; Ritchie, 2957 L.-Cpl. J.; Rongvie, 8931 J.; Smith, 2253 W.

OXFORD. AND BUCKS. L.I.—Bailey, 9782 Cpl. C.; Barley, 18951 E.; Batchelor, 10541 A. J.; Buckle, 20117 H.; Busby, 18868 H.; Collins, 19553 W.; Jordan, 17494 H. C.; Langford, 22343 N.; Law, 18687 L.-Cpl. F. T.; Mills, 19657 F.; Mosdell, 18685 W.; Mouring, 22466 E. F.; Mundy, 18758 J. E.; Simmonds, 17323 Act. Cpl. F.; Smith, 19125 I. H.; Stephenson, 9762 L.-Cpl. A.; Tasker, 11237 E. H.; Tustain, 9694 F.; Veary, 8582 L.-Cpl. R.; Wise, 10864 T.; Woodfield, 9969 A.

ESSEX R.—Adams, 19352 A.; Anderson, 2625 J.; Andrews, 24410 L.-Cpl. J.; Archer, 18439 D.; Avis, 21958 L.-Cpl. H.; Baker, 8748 L.-Cpl. S.; Ball, 16055 D.; Bareham, 18511 W.; Barker, 1481 F.; Barr, 19143 W.; Barrow, 20160 J.; Batterbee, 9652 L.-Cpl. B.; Beadle, 19669 P.; Beardwell, 20788 J.; Bearman, 9681 L.; Bentall, 19766 A.; Bidmead, 15751 L.-Cpl. L.; Boyler, 10120 D.; Bradbury, 9726 A.; Brown, 19670 J.; Bryant, 19164 C.; Bullen, 20820 C.; Bunting, 10757 C. A.; Burchett, 10310 W.; Butcher, 20773 B.; Canham, 20849 W.; Cann, 2674 E.; Cass, 9270 Sgt. W.; Chester, 19501 Sgt. E. J.; Claxton, 10848 W.; Colley, 21142 C. G.; Coote, 8672 W.; Cornish, 9940 J.; Coulson, 18611 W.; Crane, 8750 Sgt. C.; Crane, 19244 C.; Croney, 16617 P.; Cross, 7343 L.-Cpl. A.; Darnell, 13835 H.; Davis, 10738 A.; Davis, 10850 H.; Denny, 9520 C.; Dowson, 20918 L.-Cpl. J.; Diggins, 9409 G.; Downham, 18961 S.; Doyle, 10452 G.; Drane, 2271 F.; Eggleton, 17027 L.-Cpl. J.; Elsden, 19695 J.; Eustace, 9934 Sgt. R.; Eva, 19401 L.; Everett, 6109 L.-Cpl. G.; Everitt, 10337 L.-Cpl. R.; Finbow, 19630 A.; Finney, 26047 J.; Francis, 19427 W.; Free, 15908 H.; Frisby, 19382 W.; Fuller, 8576 L.-Cpl. J.; Garrett, 2112 A.; Garwood, 26859 J.; Gould, 8857 W.; Gray, 10433 W.; Green, 18949 G.; Hall, 20355 C.; Hammond, 8695 G.; Hanch, 8623 E.; Hanstock, 20112 E.; Hare, 6424 T.; Harris, 16994 A.; Harrison, 20279 F.; Hay, 8833 W.; Hayter, 20770 H.; Herbert, 10964 W.; Holden, 15312 A.; Hollis, 12650 S.; Howes, 9848 R.; Hull, 9854 A.; Jefferies, 20016 A.; Jeffrey, 19090 H.; Johnson, 10127 G.; Jolly, 20388 G.; Jones, 19723 S.; Judd, 20266 W.; King, 19286 A.; Lait, 10822 C.; Lambert, 20474 G.; Lane, 19447 L.; Leedham, 20874 F.; Leggett, 2735 Sgt. C.; Leslie, 9640 G.; Lewin, 10699 J.; Lewis, 20875 F.; Lincoln, 20765 A.; Ling, 15160 Cpl. G.; Lucy, 769 R.; McMillan, 9389 L.-Cpl. W.; Mander, 9033 L.; March, 7668 J.; Marner, 20086 L.-Cpl. F.; Mason, 9245 F.; Mayhew, 3026 H.; Melson, 8426 Sgt. T.; Miles, 20290 J.; Mitchell, 17030 H.; Mobbs, 20535 H.; Moore, 15070 B.; Morton, 8131 S.; Mortson, 10879 O.; Moss, 10033 L.-Cpl. F.; Mottram, 15025 E.; Murphy, 13020 B.; Neale, 20618 W.; Newell, 7621 E.; Nunn, 14385 E.; Ong, 10321 W.; Patient, 10298 A.; Pike, 20759 J.; Pudney, 10646 G.; Pullen, 20607 W.; Ranson, 10361 Cpl. W.; Ray, 20782 A.; Reed, 6811 F.; Richardson, 21029 W.; Richer, 9322 Cpl. A.; Rickett, 10050 L.-Cpl. W.; Roote, 19279 G.; Rose, 20253 G. W.; Rowley, 13043 Sgt. G.; Simpson, 9047 Cpl. D.; Slough, 6693 L.-Cpl. A.; Southgate, 8934 Cpl. E.; Spooner, 9644 F. G.; Staples, 20899 E.; Sturtivant, 20195 A.; Surrey, 16751 A.; Tarrant, 9224 L.-Cpl. G.; Taylor, 12193 L.-Cpl. C.; Taylor, 9797 F.; Taylor, 10333 H.; Taylor, 20125 L.-Cpl. T.; Thatcher, 8415 G.; Theedon, 19416 H.; Thorpe, 24952 A.; Thurtle, 20906 H.; Tofts, 23731 D. B.; Turner, 9337 E. C.; Tween, 16286 A.; Vinson, 16880 W.; Walker, 20239 J. W.; Warren, 20795 J. G.; Weavers, 10225 W.; Wegg, 20752 W. H.; Western, 9559 L.-Cpl. G.; Whitbread, 8534 L.-Cpl. W.; Williams, 18435 E. E.; Wiseman, 7900 W.; Wollard, 19572 J.; Woodhouse, 20911 W.; Woods, 1344 A.; Wright, 9314 Sgt. T.; Young, 9479 R.

R. BERKS R.—Adnams, 10301 G.; Allen, 15750 T. R.; Almeroth, 11930 C. W.; Alsbury, 16877 T. W.; Astron, 10785 L.-Cpl. C.; Bacon, 11171 W. J.; Berry, 16980 J.; Biddulph, 12536 E. G.; Bond, 10186 W.; Brailsford, 12925 L.-Cpl. H. F.; Brasher, 10404 F.; Brown, 10434 W. H.; Burt, 13024 D.; Chapman, 15731 T. H.; Clements, 18509 H. T.; Cornell, 25243 C.; Cox, 16716 F.; Dale, 10989 W.; Davis, 12641 W.; Day, 7426 C.; Dove, 12528 L.-Cpl. E.; Dowse, 17557 L.-Cpl. W. P.; Draycott, 11239 J.; Duffy, 17765 P.; Garwell, 15268 H. W.; Gibbons, 17647 L.-Cpl. B.; Gipp, 17481 A.; Green, 25245 P.; Griffiths, 15500 A. J.; Hall, 19600 F.; Hayley, 10215 Cpl. J. H.; Hazell, 16079 L.-Cpl. A. H.; Hollis, 10155 Sgt. P.; Hooper, 10893 T. H.; Horsman, 8739 Co. Qmr.-Sgt. A. L.; Humphries, 12560 E. J.; Inman, 12542 C.; Johnson, 17785 H.; Ling, 12068 A. W.; McClellan, 12915 L.-Cpl. W.; Martin, 12946 G. T.; Martin, 18123 L. J.; Moore, 12136 H.; Oliver, 12806 G. R.; Palmer, 17342 C. H.; Perring, 12066 E. A.; Perry, 12905 N. G.; Pierce, 15900 H. W.; Saunderson, 16691 A. R.; Scarles, 10543 L.-Cpl. A.; Shackleford, 10312 Sgt. G.; Smith, 12289 H.; Taylor, 17570 L.-Cpl. C. T.; Taylor, 10308 J.; Tegg, 12805 L.-Cpl. F.; Thackray, 12756 L.-Sgt. H. S.; Theobald, 12086 L.-Cpl. O. B.; Tillor, 18080 W.; Timms, 19607 G. T.; Turford, 12058 E.; West, 11395 T.; Wheeler, 12787 L.-Cpl. A.; White, 18612 J.; Wilkinson, 12662 L. C.; Wilcox, 12276 H. T.; Wiltshire, 19699 W. B.; Wright, 12046 C.; Young, 12893 C.

R. W. KENT R.—Aldons, 428 J.; Booker, 6619 E.; Carlton, 9001 J.; Cresswell, 718 Sgt. H.; Gumbrill, 242 C.; Harrison, 11132 A.; Heaver, 863 A.; Irving, 9051 A.; Lander, 6693 W.; Littlechild, 591 Sgt. H.; Medhurst, 397 F.; Simon, 10165 L.-Cpl. W.; Simons, 210 G.; Watson, 4111 G.

KING'S OWN (YORKS L.I.).—Ashley, 24368 A.; Allen, 19018 F. J.; Arnold, 13736 W.; Barnsley, 20091 Sgt. G. R.; Barrowclough, 24350 L.; Bartram, 18295 W.; Bell, 17537 J. H.; Britten, 13339 L.-Cpl. F.; Burrows, 21159 A.; Chapman, 21958 W.; Colgan, 15165 J. R.; Daniels, 21203 F.; Davies, 18044 H.; Doogan, 12683 J.; Egan, 25196 L.-Cpl. J. W.; Elstub, 15173 J.; Flear, 18902 A. C.; Gane, 24033 H. J.; Garner, 17013 L.; Gillard, 14420 J. A.; Gooding, 9365 C. W.; Hall, 16693 L.-Cpl. W.; Harris, 2300 W. H.; Harrison, 13425 W.; Henshaw, 3491 L.-Cpl. J.; Hewitt, 16779 F.; Hewitt, 18231 W.; Hill, 2022 G.; Hoyle, 16731 J.; Kelly, 14890 J. H.; Marsden, 24978 J. W.; Monkman, 20162 W.; Oakley, 23315 L.-Cpl. A.; O'Hara, 18680 J. H.; Oxley, 14563 L.-Cpl. G.; Parker, 17453 H.; Parkinson, 12119 P.; Pickles, 17584 A. E.; Regan, 23743 T.; Shaw, 13978 L.; Staite, 13929 G. J.; Williams, 18665 L.; Wood, 14485 O.; Wright, 10631 J.

MIDDLESEX R.—Archer, 11153 C.; Bear, 11740 F. H.; Beart, 14037 L.-Cpl. W.; Bennion, 4797 A. E.; Bradfield, 14187 Sgt. J.; Brooks, 9634 J.; Bull, 8235 F.; Carroll, 15117 Sgt. A. H.; Carter, 10358 J.; Clarke, 360 L.-Sgt. W.; Coleman, 2652 J. W.; Collins, 786 L.-Cpl. J.; Cornaby, 13083 H.; Copley, 6985 L.-Sgt. G.; Courtney, 15669 W. E.; Doble, 13204 S.; Douse, 7359 S.; Dyke, 7298 L.-Cpl. C.; Egan, 13986 L.-Cpl. C.; Field, 1285 H. J.; Finch, 19040 L.-Cpl. H.; ...

2121 L.-Cpl. A. N.; Gooch, 3699 Cpl. C. C.; Gough, 1571 D.; Gurdon, 3849 B.; Hale, 3043 W.; Hall, 4123 A. E.; Hall, 3886 T.; Hannan, 1945 M.; Harrison, 2498 E.; Hodgkiss, 17 J. C.; Hopkins, 3236 F.; Hulse, 3855 W. J.; Humphries, H. G.; Jones, 102 Co. Sgt.-Maj. A. T.; Kear, 2714 W. L.; Kel 3921 A.; Kennedy, 1889 M. T.; Lennard, 3040 J.; Lewis, 1 L.-Cpl. T.; Lewis, 2713 F. D.; Lloyd, 2601 B.; Lloyd, 2004 Lyons, 3354 E. P.; Morgan, 2855 L.-Cpl. F.; Morgan, 1936 T. Mulhalland, 3905 J.; Murphy, 2167 L.-Cpl. C.; Peart, 3844 T. Perkins, 3537 W.; Perrett, 4025 J.; Plaisted, 3640 L.-Cpl. S. Powell, 3636 W. J.; Price, 3601 T. B.; Reed, 1709 W.; Richar 3613 J.; Roderick, 3106 R.; Rogers, 2143 Sgt. N. J.; Roge 2101 Cpl. W. J.; Rosser, 3837 C.; Rudge, 1688 W.; Seary, 20 A. A. V.; Shaw, 3057 Cpl. J.; Shier, 2475 W. D.; Small, 3332 W Smith, 1784 E.; Stafford, 1619 G.; Stanbury, 3513 A. C Standerwick, 1602 W. J. C.; Taylor, 3957 F.; Toomer, 34 G. E.; Vincent, 2478 W.; Voke, 3460 T.; Watkins, 3672 Widdows, 3639 D. J.; Williams, 2454 D. J.; Wynn, 2532 L.-C T. T.; Young, 1804 H.

LONDON R.—Abberley, 4285 H.; Aiken, 2195 H. A.; All 3336 J. G.; Andrews, 3187 L.-Cpl. E.; Applegard, 3694 L.-C S. W.; Armitage, 2218 P. M.; Astill, 2615 E. W.; Atkins, 34 J. H.; Atkins, 4915 L.; Bacon, 3890 H. W.; Bailey, 4433 F. Baker, 2123 W. G.; Baratgin, 3315 Bgr. H. J.; Baron, 31 H. J. W.; Baxter, 3693 Cpl. A. E.; Beavis, 2944 L.-Cpl. Bendle, 2248 L.-Cpl. H. G.; Berry, 3011 E. E.; Bezer, 27 L.-Cpl. G.; Birbeck, 3574 A. W.; Birchmore, 5492 F.; Bi 3014 A. F.; Blew, 3589 L.-Cpl. W. W. H.; Blunt, 3425 H. Bolton, 3992 G.; Boon, 3704 S. L.; Bores, 2580 A. E.; Bowde 3297 C.; Bowman, 2098 Sgt. A. E.; Bradfield, 814 Sgt. F Brake, 3713 H. J.; Brangwin, 5657 L. M. L.; Breen, 4474 C. F Brinson, 4382 A. V.; Brooks, 3670 L.-Cpl. G. F.; Broom, 28 F. J. M.; Brown, 2911 Cpl. W. A.; Bryant, 2295 Sgt. L.; Bu 3329 L.-Cpl. P.; Bunn, 4057 C. W.; Burgess, 2374 Cpl. W. G. A Burleigh, 2823 W. C.; Burnhill, 1947 C. E.; Burt, 4155 A. V Butcher, 1939 H.; Butler, 4069 A. E.; Butt, 4418 F.; Byr 1717 L.-Cpl. D. W.; Candler, 3969 H. C.; Carden, 3081 L.-C E. C. L.; Carter, 4689 M.; Chambers, 4012 L.-Cpl. A. F Charton, 4762 J. C.; Cheale, 1279 L.-Cpl. A. W.; Chown, 2533 Clarke, 1757 T. H.; Clayton, 2082 C. C.; Clayton, 1685 G. F Cleaver, 4522 A.; Clift, 2743 J. E.; Cole, 4097 A. H Cole, 4064 L. V. P.; Collis, 4343 L. A.; Collison, 4600 F. Conner, 2098 H.; Conroy, 3357 J. H.; Coombe, 4850 G.; Coop 5499 A. G. J.; Cooper, 1592 W. S.; Cooper, 3524 W. H.; C 3932 Cpl. J.; Cox, 4799 R.; Crick, 2806 A. J.; Cripps, 28 J. L.; Crittenden, 3530 S. G.; Crockett, 4654 S. W.; Cuthbe 3625 H. A.; Dack, 3745 R. G.; Daintry, 2598 G.; Darby, 34 W. H.; Darkin, 1513 A. E.; Darnell, 4661 C. G.; Davey, 55 C.; Davis, 2720 A. J.; Davis, 3621 L.-Cpl. E. J.; Dawson, 36 H.; Dennis, 3641 E. A.; Dixon, 3850 L.-Cpl. C.; Dixon, 28 L.-Cpl. R. M.; Dobson, 3459 R.; Dunble, 5586 A. C.; Durst 3171 A. J.; Earthy, 4329 W.; East, 2545 F.; Enticknap, 10 H. J.; Escott, 4034 A. E.; Fennell, 3302 W. C.; Flanag 3663 J. F. J.; Flatt, 2769 L. A.; Floyed, 3549 G. A.; Fontai 3918 A. B.; Foreman, 2460 G. L.; Freeman, 4005 A. E. J.; Fren 4130 J. J.; Frier, 4360 R. E.; Garratt, 5273 A. N.; Gibbo 3993 F. A.; Goodall, 4086 G. R. E.; Goodard, 4948 S.; Goo hind, 3922 J.; Goodridge, 4231 A. H.; Goundry, 3509 T. Gray, 2241 L.-Cpl. C. F.; Green, 5810 J. W.; Griffen, 1626 A. Griswood, 3518 W.; Gubbins, 2535 Cpl. S. P.; Halford, 45 F. C.; Hall, 3741 G. G.; Handscombe, 2053 W.; Hamlin, 40 W. F.; Harding, 3566 A. J.; Harland, 2577 C. G.; Harris, 45 G. H.; Harris, 5515 J. H.; Harrison, 1512 Cpl. E. C.; Harro 4513 Cpl. S. H.; Hart, 4602 A. W.; Hartnell, 3395 W. J.; Ha 2120 L.; Hassett, 2565 Sgt. E. E.; Hatley, 380 S.; Hawkl 2122 F.; Hawthorn, 4286 S. J.; Hellier, 3465 E. W.; Heronim 2840 J. A.; Herring, 1831 R. S.; Hillman, 5520 T. W.; Ho garth, 3755 W. E. T.; Hole, 4924 E. A.; Holloway, 1817 L.-C H. V.; Holtz, 2258 P. M.; Horsey, 2987 Act. Sgt. F. L. G Howard, 4542 F. A.; Howard, 3634 P. R.; Howell, 3342 J.; Ho lett, 4767 D. H.; Humphrey, 3624 W. C. B.; Hussey, 5924 F. Hutchings, 3262 Sgt. E.; Hutchings, 3847 H. J.; Hutt, 28 L.-Cpl. B. B.; Hynds, 1540 F.; Jackson, 3143 Cpl. H. E.; Je 4415 F. W.; Jenkins, 3053 L.-Cpl. F. W.; Jewiss, 4001 H. W. Jeynes, 2982 A. G. H.; Johnson, 4891 R. H. H.; Jones, 45 F. C.; Jones, 4095 K.; Jones, 4698 S. J.; Jones, 5587 W. J. Joyce, 4342 J. H.; Kemp, 5004 F.; Kemp, 3640 T. H.; Kirl 1485 L.-Cpl. G. H. E.; Lacey, 2675 G. H.; Lambert, 4909 C Lambert, 3905 S.; Lawrence, 2692 H. R.; Leith, 2090 L. A Leonard, 4684 W.; Lester, 2749 A. E.; Lewis, 3783 Sgt. T. S Lott, 2581 L.-Cpl. T. R.; Loveridge, 2092 A. L.; Lucas, 45 F.; McCarthy, 3515 J.; Macolino, 4348 F. H.; Macrow, 3 C Qmr.-Sgt. J.; Maddaford, 5589 H. J.; Madger, 2573 L.-C A. W.; Mahoney, 1937 J. W.; Maidment, 155 Cpl. A. S.; M riott, 1877 L.-Cpl. F. G.; Merrick, 1302 R. G.; Murch, 20 Sgt. C. E.; Murray, 3000 E. F.; Merriman, 4913 J. W.; Mill 2002 L.-Sgt. S.; Mills, 3771 S. F.; Mitchell, 3328 J.; Mogrid 3440 S.; Money, 1317 Sgt. E. G.; Moon, 3456 C. L.; Moo 4372 P. F.; Moulden, 3931 C. W.; Moyise, 4617 F. J.; Nea 2145 W. A.; Newham, 1651 C. F.; Noakes, 2634 V. F.; Nol 4519 W.; Olley, 4731 W. T. P.; Packer, 1771 F. J.; Parget 2758 R. W.; Parker, 4505 H. M.; Parkins, 4388 H. A.; Pest 4665 A. E.; Phillips, 3027 R. W.; Philo, 4417 G. E.; Pickerir 1816 R. C.; Pidgeon, 4603 W. J.; Pike, 3260 C. J.; Pind 4811 A. W.; Pink, 4102 E. W.; Playfair, 1879 V. H.; Ponsfor 3808 H.; Poole, 5053 D. H.; Price, 2227 W. R. J.; Prin 3137 L.-Sgt. G.; Pringle, 4635 J.; Pudleyn, 1061 Co. Sgt.-M E. H.; Quirk, 1952 W. P.; Reeves, 4077 L. G.; Reeve, 28 V. H.; Reid, 3577 G.; Richardson, 3225 J. F.; Riordar 1723 Sgt. W. R.; Robbins, 2506 V. E.; Robertson, 3850 A. I Robinson, 4717 A. L.; Ruston, 5006 T. A.; Saddleton, 30 Act. Cpl. S.; Sanders, 1713 H. V.; Saw, 4838 F. G.; Seel 3031 Sgt. J. C.; Seymour, 1716 S. W.; Sharpe, 3421 L. A Sheppard, 3611 J. T.; Sherratt, 1783 Sgt. H. H.; Shilst 1427 C. T.; Sim, 1471 Sgt. C. K.; Simpson, 4792 J. M. M Sims, 3775 L.-Cpl. W. R. L.; Skinner, 1961 Cpl. S. A. T.; Skipp 5581 R. L.; Small, 3845 P. H.; Smith, 5540 F.; Smith, 34 F. J.; Smith, 2948 H. G.; Smith, 3093 L.-Cpl. H. R.; Smit 4349 R. W.; Smith, 3735 W. H.; Smith, 4373 W. L.; Spence 4518 H. F.; Spicer, 3343 W. R.; Spooner, 3201 T. C.; Spurg 3691 W. S.; Squires, 2101 A. W.; Stears, 3325 S. G.; Stevenso 3372 A.; Stocker, 3807 E.; Stockman, 1886 R.; Streath 1662 W. A.; Stringer, 5563 G. O.; Stroud, 2005 R. J Sutch, 3091 H. A.; Sweet, 3341 H. E.; Syrett, 2943 H. C Tacon, 5201 E. N.; Tate, 3944 H. H.; Taylor, 1739 L.-Sg G. W.; Telfer, 2361 Sgt. G. F.; Thurgate, 4135 R. L.; Trick 2599 W.; Trineman, 4737 J.; Trussell, 3248 W. H.; Tolch 5045 C. R.; Tomblin, 1872 J. R.; Toone, 3989 C. L.; Town end, 4576 G.; Tuck, 2171 C. C.; Turner, 3703 C. J.; Turne 3763 H. S.; Turner, 3702 L.-Cpl. W. F.; Upton, 4051 C. A Underdown, 4409 H. P.; Valentine, 4724 F.; Wakeford, 42

3.7.16

Dear Mrs. Nevill,

    I hardly know how to begin to write this letter at all. It seems almost an impertinence to try to sympathise with you in such a dreadful loss, but I feel it my duty to tell you how your son Capt. Nevill met his death. He was in command of one of our leading Companies in the attack on Montauban on the 1st of this month, and led his company most gallantly and with the utmost coolness up to the German front line trench, where he was shot. Death must have been absolutely instantaneous. He was one of the bravest men I have ever met, and was loved and trusted by his men to such a degree that they would have followed him anywhere, and did follow him that morning through an inferno of shell, rifle and machine gun fire. We feel his loss most deeply as a brother officer, who was not only the life and soul of the mess, but also a most capable and fearless soldier. He started his company in the assault by kicking off a football which his men dribbled right up to the German trench. I have been able to get that ball since, and will of course send it to you if you should want it as a memento of him, but I and all the other officers of the Battalion would be very grateful to you if you would allow us to keep it as a regimental trophy, and in memory of your son's gallantry. We have recovered his body and have buried him in Carnoy cemetery with our six other officers who were killed.

    We have put a heavy wooden cross on the grave with their names on it, and at the end of the war will put a permanent memorial there.

    Yours sincerely,

      A. P. B. Irwin

        (Major Cmdg 8th Batt. E Surrey Reg.)

A letter held in the archives of the Imperial War Museum.

'You shall swear that you shall keep the Peace of our Lord the King well and lawfully according to your power, and shall arrest all those who shall make any contest, riot, debate, or affray, in breaking of the said peace, and shall bring them into the house or Compter of one of the Sheriffs. And if you shall be withstood by strength of such misdoers, you shall raise upon them hue and cry [and] shall follow them from street to street and from ward to ward until they are arrested. And also you shall search at all times when you shall be required by scavenger or Bedel, for the common nuisances of the ward; until they are arrested. . . . And the faults you shall find, you shall present them unto the mayor and to the officers of the said City. . . . So God help you and the Saints.'

An extract from The Parish Constable's Oath, *which was based on the medieval* Liber Albus.

LIST 3 (continued)
PERSONS NOT ELIGIBLE FOR JURY SERVICE

MENTALLY DISORDERED PERSONS

A person who suffers or has suffered from mental illness, psychopathic disorder, mental handicap or severe mental handicap and on account of that condition either:-

    (a) is resident in a hospital or other similar institution; or

    (b) regularly attends for treatment by a medical practitioner.

A person for the time being in guardianship under section 33 of the Mental Health Act 1959 or section 37 of the Mental Health Act 1983. A person who has been determined by a judge to be incapable, by reason of mental disorder, of managing and administering his property and affairs.

(In this Group:-

    (a) 'mental handicap' means a state of arrested or incomplete development of mind (not amounting to severe mental handicap) which includes significant impairment of intelligence and social functioning;

    (b) 'severe mental handicap' means a state of arrested or incomplete development of mind which includes severe impairment of intelligence and social functioning;

    (c) other expressions are to be construed in accordance with the said Act.)

If you are in any doubt as to whether this section applies to you, you should consult your doctor.

Extract from the Jury Summons Form, No. 5221, issued by The Lord Chancellor's Department.

COURT No. 13

ON	TURESAY 14 OCTOBER 1986
BEFORE	HIS HONOUR JUDGE PETRE
AT	9.30

FOR APPLICATION ONLY

IN CHAMBERS

DEFENDANTS NOT TO ATTEND
WITNESSES NO TO ATTEND

ROBERT WILLIAM KENNEDY   861360

SEAN MILLARD   861393

THE ABOVE CASES ARE LISTED FOR APPLICATION FOR BAIL

10.00

IN OPEN COURT

FOR TRIAL

1   LARRY ERNEST JONES   860216
     KEVIN MICHAEL JAMIE THATCHER

part heard

BONFIRE PRAYERS

Remember, remember the fifth of November
The Gunpowder Treason and Plot,
I see no reason why Gunpowder Treason,
Should ever be forgot.

Guy Fawkes, Guy Fawkes 'twas his intent
To blow up the King and the Parliament,
Three score barrels of powder below,
Poor old England to overthrow.

By God's providence he was catched
With a dark lantern and burning match.
Holloa boys, holloa boys, ring bells ring,
Holloa boys, holloa boys, God save the King.

A penny loaf to feed old Pope,
A farthing cheese to choke him,
A pint of beer to rinse it down,
A Faggot of sticks to burn him.

Burn him in a tub of tar,
Burn him like a blazing star,
Burn his body from his head,
Then we'll say old Pope is dead.

Hip Hip hoorah!
Hip Hip hoorah!
Hip Hip hoorah!

God Rest You Merry Gentlemen

SALE STARTS
28 DEC

But while bravery and service to the community are recognised by honours and awards, there are many ways in which people can make good news. Success in industry and commerce, for instance, creates the wealth that provides so many of the things that make life happier and more comfortable. It is not just the big companies with household names; quite small companies with only a few members can make a very significant contribution to the prosperity of their communities.

The people in Britain who have helped their companies to success also come to the Palace as winners of The Queen's Awards for Export and Technology.

For example, last year there was a firm with only five employees, who make darts and export them to no less than forty countries! They were so enterprising that they introduced the game of darts into places where it had never been played.

Then there were the consulting engineers who won their Award for technological achievement for their ingenious work on the Thames Flood Barrier.

A small Scottish firm with eighteen employees make a product so good that they have sold their heating systems even in the United States and West Germany

Another firm has scored a rare double with their magnets for medical scanners, winning both the Awards - for Export and for Technology.

There are masses more, and it is encouraging to know that again next year there will be a new group coming to receive their awards, whose achievements will be just as ingenious and just as exciting. There are similar examples throughout the Commonwealth. These success stories are often pushed into the background but they are the guarantee of our future. Christmas is a time of good news. I believe it is a time to look at the good things of life and to remember that there are a great many people trying to make the world a better place, even though their efforts may go unrecognised.

There is a lesson in this for us all and we should
never forget our obligation to make our own individual
contributions, however small, towards the sum of human goodness.
The story of the Good Samaritan reminds us of our duty to our
neighbour. We should try to follow Christ's clear instruction
at the end of that story: "Go and do thou likewise".

I wish you all a very happy Christmas and I hope that
we shall all try to make some good news in the coming year.

Extract from The Queen's Christmas Message to the Commonwealth in 1985, reprinted with the kind permission of Her Majesty The Queen.

Cin: To the dairy in the next street - come along.
Butt: Coming.(theyexit)(enter Claribelle.)
Clar: All clear nobody about. Now for a drop of oh be joyful.(goes
      to Inn door, interrupted by   the chorus, she goes centre
      I'll try again. Never   thi   hout an effort.
      (repeat bus: by anothe   ain, Ah well
      I'll try again present   happy today
      I think perhaps I ha   s tried hard enough
      but there you neve   ing about getting off
      I must tell you a   .I once walked out with
          Song.........   Buttons enters - he
      watches Claribelle)
Clar: Now to try again(looks fur   round   s into Inn)
Butt:(coming C) The sly ol   ale   wa   ing to the dai
      to get the cat som   that   eds the milk-
      MILK STOUT. But th   ke an engine she won't
      go unless she's w   omes.
Clar:(coming from Inn)   again soon.
Butt: Now to surprise h   : C ar...Puss ...Puss..
Clar: You, you little p
Butt: Have you got the   Claribelle?
Clar: Of course I have   k - you nasty little spy.
Butt: Does the cat drin   uiness.
Clar: No, but I do.
Butt: What about a sip.
Clar: Sorry, but its half   or me.
Butt: Go on just a teeny w   our half.
Clar: Can't be done.
Butt: Why not?
Clar: Cause my half's on t
Butt: Done again.(Lasilena   age)
Lena: Claribelle, where ar
Clar: Thats my dear sister   Lena enters)
Lena: There you are darli   or you everywhere
      I have some good ne
Clar: Oh do tell me, I'm   the stage)
Lena: Yes, I've noticed t
Clar: What did you say?
Lena: Oh nothing darling   have ju heard that the Prince is
      giving a ball at th   ace ton   t for all the local gentry.
Clar: Thats us - we are su   to be i ted and I have'nt a thing to
      wear.
Lena: What about your pig kin   with sewer rat.
Clar: But that's out of d   dar   have new dresses for th
      ball.
Lena: I will have a dress   ook younger.
Butt: .Why not try monkey lands?
Lena: You rude boy I'll box your ears.

n: The pleasure is all mine sweet child.
: Are you the Prince Charming?
n: My name is Dandini, the Prince's adjutant. May I ask your
  name pretty one.
: I am Cinderella the step daughter of the Baron de Broke.
n: The Baron must be a proud man to own such a beautiful daughter.
: The Baron thinks far more of his own daughters Claribelle and
  Lasilena.
n: Are the just as beautiful as you?
: That you must find out for yourself sir.
n: Do you believe in love at the first sight Cinderella?
: I cannot say for I have never be   in love.
n: Surely then you have'nt seen m   he world.
: I have not- but my step-siste
n: Have they ever been to the Ro
: No - The Baron says they must   ing out party first.
n: Thank goodness for that. Tell   lla have you ever had
  a dream lover?
: Yes I have a dream lover.
n: What is he like?
: He is tall, rich and hands
n: Like me perchance?
: Yes very like you- Oh I s   said   uch.
            Duet.........Cind   ne Pri
: I hear the Prince is givi   all t   ht.
  I should love to go. Cou   y get me an
  invitation?
n: Yes I'm sure I could ma   one condition.
: And the condition is?
n: That you dance only wi
: But what if the Prin   with me. Don't you
  think he would be   yed
n. No I don't   the Prin
: Alright   case I pr   ron with Lady Sylvia)
: How   top talking   en Cinderella. Have you
  finis   shopping you   se   do?(Prince whispers in
  Lady   's ear)
: Yes pa   I have finished the
: Have I not told you not to c   m   pa in public.
: Yes Papa.
: There you go again how dare
: I am very sorry.
: Go home and prepare th   dy Sylvia and I. We will
  come on later. Hurry.
n: May I walk home with you Cinderella?
: You may not young man.(exit Cinders) Now sir who are you and
  what do you mean by talking to my step-daughter?
: This is Dandini, the Prince's adjutant.

Wills

Sir Leonard Hutton, of Kingston upon Thames, Surrey, the Yorkshire and England cricketer, left estate valued at £382,313 net.

Mr Walter Spender Dingwall, of Henfield, West Sussex, Headmaster of Hurstpierpoint College 1937-45, Chichester Diocesan Secretary 1946-61, left estate valued at £1,948,379 net. He left £3,125 to the World Wildlife Fund, £1,250 to the Friends of Chichester Cathedral and to the RSPB, and £625 to Chichester Diocesan Fund and Board of Finance.

Thomas Arthur, third Baron Ponsonby of Shulbrede, of London SE11, Chief Opposition Whip in the House of Lords 1982-90, left estate valued at £270,078 net.

Mr Ronald Ivan Norreys Greaves, of Cambridge, Emeritus Professor of Pathology at Cambridge University, who pioneered the production of dried plasma and organised the first blood transfusion service, left estate valued at £176,219 net.

Mr Howard Poulsom Forder, of Curbar, Derbyshire, a Past Master Cutler, formerly a director of Arthur Lee, the steel company, and previously a British Steel Corporation executive, and Pro-Chancellor of Sheffield University, left estate valued at £305,641 net. He left £1,000 to Curbar Parish Council.

Brigadier Cuthbert Goulburn DSO retd, of Bridgnorth, Shropshire, who commanded the 8th King's Royal Irish Hussars in North Africa and north-west Europe during the Second World War, and later served as a military attaché in Egypt and Spain, Hon Colonel of the Shropshire Yeomanry 1962-73, left estate valued at £2,850,688 net. He left £40,000 to the Queen's Royal Irish Hussars Benevolent Fund.

Sir John Christopher Blake Richmond KCMG, of Durham, former Ambassador to Kuwait and the Sudan, and lecturer in Modern Near East History at the School of Oriental Studies, Durham University, 1966-74, left estate valued at £120,139 net.

Brigadier Patrick Miles Pennington Hobson DSO retd, of Puttenham, Surrey, left estate valued at £108,263 net.

Mr Jack Favill Redfern, of Cerne Abbas, Dorset, the journalist, who worked for nearly 50 years with the *Daily Express*, left estate valued at £99,367 net. He left £100 to the Society of St Francis, Hilfield, Cerne Abbas.

The Hon Henry Lovell Tennant, of London SW2, left estate valued at £3,264,072 net.

Mr John Anthony Forster Blight, of Callington, Cornwall, solicitor, left estate valued at £1,877,735 net. He left £2,000 to King George's Fund for Sailors.

Mr Ronald Edward John Hepburn, of Buckland, Surrey, left estate valued at £1,285,542 net.

Mr William Henry Cecil Hutchinson, of Weston, Lincolnshire, left estate valued at £2,082,677 net.

Mrs Anny Ledsam, of Birmingham, left estate valued at £1,130,431 net.

Mr Gilbert Wilson Nicholson, of Windermere, Cumbria, left estate valued at £1,006,795 net. He left £1,000 to Ambleside Health Centre, for the purchase of equipment and a further £4,000 to be divided equally between the doctors there.

Miss Margaret Max Spencer, of Branksome, Dorset, left estate valued at £922,157 net. After personal bequests of £11,100, she left £2,000 each to the Friends of both Salisbury and Exeter Cathedrals, £1,000 each to Queen Margaret's School, York, James Allen's Girls School, East Dulwich, London, and Help the Aged; £500 each to St Philip and All Saints Church, North Sheen, Surrey, and the USPG; £250 to the Dorset Naturalists Trust; £100 to St Aldhelm's Church, Branksome; £250 to the National Trust, Dorset Centre; and the residue to the National Trust.

Marjorie Greenwood, of Inkberrow, Worcestershire, left estate valued at £132,293 net. She left some effects to personal legatees, £8,000 to Trustees for maintenance of any dog in her ownership, and the residue of her estate equally between the National Canine Defence League, Barnardo's and National Children's Home.

Extract from the Independent, *Saturday 24 November 1990.*

ILLUSTRATIONS

(In the order they appear in the book)

The flag of St. George
Win through
Walking the dog
Severe weather
Hunting
D' ye ken John Peel?
Springtime
Crufts
The Dogs Home, Battersea
Bingo
The telephone
Sea-angling
Cambridge University
The Chelsea Flower Show
The Country Gentlemen's Association
Harley Street
The tabloids
The newsagent's
Press release
Traffic
Roadworks
Roadworks End
Sea-fever
Shipping forecast
Cross-Channel ferry
If the invader comes
Chinese restaurant
Sellafield
Weather comments
Tennis
Test cricket
Beach cricket

Glyndebourne
The garden
An auction
A county wedding
Nanny
Summer
The Royal Garden Party
Shooting
Bradford
The Last Night of the Proms
Preparatory school
State school
Nature trail
Hotting
Industry
Parliamentary election
The Houses of Parliament
The House of Lords
The Battle of the Somme
A letter to Mrs Nevill
On the beat
Jury duties
Court No. 13
Bonfire night
God Rest You Merry Gentlemen
Christmas shopping
The Queen's Christmas Message
A sea-side pavilion
Pantomime
Wills
Christmas comments
The One Great Scorer

ACKNOWLEDGMENTS

The author and the publisher gratefully acknowledge the help of those listed below in granting permission to use material still in copyright in the book.

Crufts Roll of Honour, reproduced by kind permission of the Kennel Club.

The Battersea Dogs Home register and letterhead reproduced by kind permission of the Dogs Home, Battersea.

'How to pass and receive a telephone call' reproduced by kind permission of the BT Museum.

Rupert Brooke's parody of Housman's 'A Shropshire Lad' first appeared in the *Saturday Westminster, 1911.*

Extract from the Chelsea Flower Show Official Catalogue 1990, reproduced by kind permission of the Royal Horticultural Society.

Extract from *Country* magazine and the CGA logo reproduced by kind permission of the Country Gentlemen's Association.

'Reach for the new Sun...' reproduced by kind permission of the British Library.

AA Roadwatch, reproduced by kind permission of the Automobile Association.

'Sorry for any delay...' sign reproduced by kind permission of the Department of Transport.

'Sea-fever' reproduced by kind permission of the Society of Authors as the literary representative of the Estate of John Masefield.

Shipping Forecast - this material is Crown Copyright and is reproduced by kind permission of the Controller of HMSO.

'If The Invader Comes' - this material is Crown Copyright and is reproduced by kind permission of the Central Office of Information.

Extract from Law 17 of *The Laws of Cricket* reproduced by kind permission of the members of the Marylebone Cricket Club. Law 17:7 continues -
(d) In the event of an innings being completed and a new innings commencing during the last hour of the match, the number of overs to be bowled in the new innings shall be calculated on the basis of one 6-ball over for every three minutes or part thereof remaining for play (or one 8-ball over for every four minutes or part thereof remaining for play); or alternatively on the basis that sufficient overs be bowled to enable the full minimum quota of overs to be completed under circumstances governed by (a), (b) and (c) above. In all such cases the alternative which allows the greater number of overs shall be employed.

Extract from Harwood House Catalogue, reproduced by kind permission of Christie's.

'Wedding Issue' design by kind permission of *Country Life* magazine.

Extract from *Nanny Says* by Sir Hugh Casson and Joyce Grenfell, reproduced by kind permission of Souvenir Press.

Extract from *Bradford, a Travel Guide* reproduced by kind permission of Bradford Council's Economic Development Unit.

Extract from *Quest for Prosperity* by Konusuke Matsushita reproduced by kind permission of the PHP Institute, Inc.

Extract from *Vacher's Parliamentary Companion*, reproduced by kind permission of Vacher's Publications.

Extract from *The Times* reporting the Battle of the Somme, reproduced by kind permission of the British Library.

Extract from *Billie:The Nevill Letters* by kind permission of the Imperial War Museum. *Billie:The Nevill Letters* are published by Julia MacRae Ltd, an imprint of Random House UK Ltd.

Extract from the Jury Summons Form - this material is Crown Copyright and is reproduced by kind permission of the Controller of HMSO.

Extract from The Queen's Christmas Message to the Commonwealth in 1985, reproduced by kind permission of Her Majesty The Queen.

And particular thanks to John Beard for providing us with the Bingo Lingo. Also thanks to Dennis Hopper.

In accordance with Section 57 of the Copyright Designs and Patents Act 1988 the publishers have made every effort to contact the author, the author's estate or the source of the following material reproduced in this book: a poem entitled 'Hearts of Oak', a poem entitled 'When the One Great Scorer...', a poem entitled 'Win Through', an untitled poem about grouse shooting by W. Carter Platts, a poem entitled 'Bonfire Prayer', an extract from a pantomime script and an extract from 'The Union Jack Book'. In the event that these works are still in copyright and that the copyright owners can be determined, the publishers shall be pleased to clear the copyright in the usual way.